# The Right to Teach

# The Right to Teach

*Creating Spaces for Teacher Agency*

Alcione Negrão Ostorga

ROWMAN & LITTLEFIELD
Lanham • Boulder • New York • London

Published by Rowman & Littlefield
An imprint of The Rowman & Littlefield Publishing Group, Inc.
4501 Forbes Boulevard, Suite 200, Lanham, Maryland 20706
www.rowman.com

Unit A, Whitacre Mews, 26-34 Stannary Street, London SE11 4AB

Copyright © 2018 by Alcione Negrão Ostorga

*All rights reserved.* No part of this book may be reproduced in any form or by any electronic or mechanical means, including information storage and retrieval systems, without written permission from the publisher, except by a reviewer who may quote passages in a review.

British Library Cataloguing in Publication Information Available

**Library of Congress Cataloging-in-Publication Data**

Names: Ostorga, Alcione Negrão, 1952- author.
Title: The right to teach : creating spaces for teacher agency / Alcione Negrão Ostorga.
Description: Lanham, Maryland : Rowman & Littlefield, [2018] | Includes bibliographical references and index.
Identifiers: LCCN 2018004374 (print) | LCCN 2018017074 (ebook) | ISBN 9781475834505 (electronic) | ISBN 9781475834482 (cloth: alk. paper) | ISBN 9781475834499 (pbk. : alk. paper)
Subjects: LCSH: Teaching, Freedom of. | Teachers—Professional relationships. | Teacher participation in curriculum planning.
Classification: LCC LC72 (ebook) | LCC LC72 .O77 2018 (print) | DDC 370.21—dc23
LC record available at https://lccn.loc.gov/2018004374

∞ ™ The paper used in this publication meets the minimum requirements of American National Standard for Information Sciences Permanence of Paper for Printed Library Materials, ANSI/NISO Z39.48-1992.

Printed in the United States of America

# Contents

| | |
|---|---|
| Acknowledgments | vii |
| Introduction | ix |

**Part I: Agency in the Teaching Profession**

| | | |
|---|---|---|
| 1 | What Is Teacher Agency? | 3 |
| 2 | A Sociohistorical Look at the Loss of Teacher Agency | 13 |
| 3 | A Theoretical Framework for Promoting Teacher Agency | 25 |

**Part II: Teacher Agency in Practice**

| | | |
|---|---|---|
| 4 | Teacher Agency: One Teacher's Journey<br>*Lileana Ríos-Ledezma* | 43 |
| 5 | How Can Teachers Exercise Agency? | 57 |
| 6 | How Can Teacher Educators and School Leaders Support Teacher Agency? | 69 |

| | |
|---|---|
| References | 89 |
| Index | 95 |
| About the Author and Contributor | 97 |

# Acknowledgments

The creation of this book has not been a solitary process, and I want to thank the many friends and colleagues who helped me to complete the work through their willingness to read the manuscripts and to dialogue with me about the complexities of the ideas presented. Specifically, I want to thank the many colleagues who read the manuscripts and provided me with valuable feedback. Among these, I thank my friend and colleague Martha Tevis for her expertise and suggestions on the history of the teaching profession; Maria Cristina Villarreal for her perspectives as a teacher leader; Alejandro Garcia and Jesus Abrego for their insights as educators of school administrators; and Joan Wink, who has inspired me through her wonderful books and presentations about critical pedagogy and teachers' work and who reviewed the entire book manuscript, giving me valuable advice to help me make the book more engaging and reader friendly.

I also want to give a very special thank-you to Lileana Ríos-Ledezma, author of chapter 4, who has been my student, protégé, and friend. Her numerous narratives and accounts of her practices as a teacher have been the key inspiration in the creation of this book. It would not have been possible without her incredible strength as a teacher who achieved agency because of her skillfulness and focus on what was best for her students.

# Introduction

"As a teacher, I have learned that unpacking the 'facts' with a community of unique and critical eyes is essential to engaging learners and allowing learning to unfold. I am also aware that this kind of teaching leaves me feeling vulnerable because the lesson plan is never finalized. The direction and depth of the learning are as diverse as each of my students. True to life, there is no manual with all the answers. The 'answers' are shaped by the direction we take as a learning community. Most important, we come to realize that the answers are not as important as the process we take to discover them."—Stinson, 2005, p. 105

This quote comes from one of the teacher-contributors to the book edited by Sonia Nieto (2005), *Why We Teach*. It helps us to remember that teaching requires the skills and talent to make decisions on our feet. Yes, planning is crucial, but so is the teacher's willingness to modify those plans at a moment's notice—an important element to facilitate the learning process based on the myriad unexpected responses to our teaching acts.

Implied by Stinson is also the fact that our teaching acts should not be limited to the minute detailed objectives in our lesson plans but should also include the unexpected and how learning specific details is connected to the whole individual (i.e., each student) in our classrooms. The connections are as varied as the relationships between each fact or story plot and the relationships to the values and cultures in the lives of each student. For this reason, the act of teaching must include the space for decision making.

Teaching has historically been characterized by contradicting perspectives. On the one hand, it is considered important and laudable. In effect, teachers are often called superheroes because they play a key role in the development of children, guiding them toward adulthood. Many have looked up to teachers as role models and praise them for the many sacrifices they make for the benefit of their students. Others say they "wear many hats," as they play many roles in the lives of their students, sometimes as advocates, counselors, cheerleaders, or captains in their classrooms. On the other hand, teaching is sometimes not considered so important a profession, if it is considered a profession at all.

The media certainly does not promote a positive image of teachers. While there are some examples of model teachers who have facilitated success in their students in apparently miraculous ways, such as Mr. Escalante in the movie *Stand and Deliver* (Musca and Menendez, 1988) and Erin Grunwell in the movie *Freedom Writers* (LaGravenese, 2007), a great deal of negative publicity comes from news about the rare cases of unethical teachers who have been convicted of helping their students cheat on standardized tests (Brown, 2015). Or worse yet are the cases of teachers who became sexually involved with their students. Some recent movies that have contributed to negative images of teachers are the documentary *Waiting for Superman* (Chilcott and Guggenheim, 2010) and *Bad Teacher* (Miller, Householter, and Kasdan, 2011), which as a comedy is not meant to be taken seriously but nevertheless perpetuates negative images of the teaching profession.

Thus, teachers generally have been blamed for the ills of education (Walker, 2014, September). Certainly the No Child Left Behind (NCLB) Act focused not only on the performance of schools but also ultimately on the performance of teachers through only one measure, the results of their students' performances on standardized tests. Though NCLB was replaced by the Every Student Succeeds Act (ESSA) in 2015, which moves away from the excessive federal control on schools, its effects will most certainly take a long time to wane.

The implication has been that, if students do not learn, it is the teacher's fault. This is as ludicrous as believing that, if a patient fails to heal, it is the doctor who is at fault. Sometimes this may be the case, if the doctor is unethical or incompetent. However, usually it is because illnesses, especially severe ones, are complex imbalances in the body that may not be curable, depending on severity and the overall health of the patient. Why is it not possible to realize that teaching is similar? Certainly, some teachers are incompetent and unethical, but all professions have incompetent and unethical behavior. What is always true is that learning depends on a variety of factors, which include the home environment, family conditions, socioemotional circumstances, and cognitive abilities, just to name a few.

Although there are numerous reasons students do poorly on standardized tests, teachers are typically blamed for their performance. Often, when the government funnels monies into school districts to improve conditions and provide extra resources, a great portion is spent on professional development. Therein lies the assumption that teachers are not well prepared and need special training to improve their teaching practices. After receiving special training in the form of instruction on the latest curriculum model or instructional approach, teachers are policed to ensure fidelity to what they were taught. And so, the teaching profession has increasingly become an occupation, or simply a job and not a profession.

While educators argue that teaching is a profession and this concept is a major focus among teacher educator's work, it is not often treated as such because of the oversimplification and undervaluing of the knowledge of the teacher by the general public. Like a profession, teaching requires formal, specialized training to be applied in the service to others for pay. However, professions, such as doctors, lawyers, and engineers, also are generally associated with prestige.

Teaching lacks this level of prestige because it is mistakenly conceptualized as easy. Teaching also lacks the degree of autonomy normally associated with professions, and teachers continue to lose the little autonomy they once had. Teachers, mostly public employees throughout the ages, have exercised some degree of autonomy in their classrooms within the organizational structures of public schooling. Yet, the degree of autonomy has decreased drastically over the past decades.

While teacher educators in academia have continuously worked to raise the professional standards of teaching, educational policies have converted it into a technical occupation, with teachers treated like technicians. The differences between professionals and technicians lies primarily in the level of autonomy allowed. While professionals make decisions about approaches and methods depending on the specific contexts of the moment, technicians apply specific methods and skills as mandated by their supervisors. They are not expected or allowed to make decisions in their work.

Technical jobs require the application of skills with inanimate objects. On the other hand, teachers work with complex, living human beings still in the process of development who possess a variety of cultures, languages, abilities, and personalities. A simplistic linear means-ends approach does not fit in this context. What is most alarming is that the educational policies responsible for transforming teaching into a technical job have been created by politicians who do not have the kind of expertise teachers have. No wonder teacher attrition has become a topic of concern (Long, 2015), as the teaching force with expertise derived from experience dwindles.

As technicians, teachers are generally expected to follow prescribed curricula and specific approaches in instruction mandated by the school and district administrators in a top-down fashion. The accountability movement in the implementation of NCLB, with its emphasis on alignment of instruction, has veered toward an emphasis on standardization that permeates not only school districts but also entire states and the whole country. This is evident in the latest fad promoted at the national level, the Common Core State Standards, with the aim of equalizing the curriculum for every child in the country. Though criticized as being founded on faulty research (Gamson, Lu, and Eckert, 2013) and failing to take into consideration the learning needs of such special populations as English language learners (TESOL International Association, 2013), it has been adopted by 42 states and the District of Columbia (*U.S. News*, 2015).

Some level of standardization is desirable so that basic content knowledge is taught to all and children can become contributors to society at large. But, should the content taught in all schools be equal? Or should there be variations according to the context of local communities? Can we envision schools where the content taught is meaningful to the variety of students who receive it? If so, should we not seek to promote culturally relevant teaching, as well as core knowledge?

If we value individuality, creativity, and critical thinking, then there must be spaces for different kinds of teaching to achieve similar purposes. Within this context, teachers as professionals can apply their expertise to engage diverse learners and lead them toward becoming knowledgeable, critical thinkers and contributors to our society. Instead, they are treated as technicians who are expected to follow prescribed methods and content mindlessly, without regard to who their students are or the specific contexts of their classrooms.

Though the current policies are being questioned, generally the quality of a teacher's work is solely measured by standardized test results, which merely measure students' ability to interpret the questions asked. These tests do not measure students' ability to think critically or to make decisions based on values and ethics. Nor do they assess the creativity and inventiveness necessary to create innovative ways of working and living in an ever-changing society.

This book presents a theoretical model for the promotion of teacher autonomy, or teacher agency. This framework allows teachers to make professional decisions in their classrooms, within the context of the school systems currently in place. This would require a complete transformation of the archetype of teacher as it now exists in the United States and in many nations across the world.

I propose that teachers ought to be respected for their knowledge, experience, and commitment to teach our nation's students. Despite the fact that they are the most knowledgeable about the specific needs and contexts of their classrooms, in the current environment, they are not afforded the space to make the most appropriate decisions for their classrooms, so they have no autonomy. Yet, autonomy does not quite fit the context of the teaching profession. Instead, I propose that teachers be afforded agency to act professionally, to engage in and lead inquiry, and to make decisions based on their analysis and expertise of the art and science of teaching.

*Introduction*

## AGENCY OR AUTONOMY

What is autonomy? In many ways, the term *autonomy* may be inappropriate for the teaching profession because the nature of teaching does not truly allow teachers to be autonomous. To promote teacher autonomy, the teaching profession would need to be organized in a very different way from how it functions now. For instance, the teacher, perhaps, could be self-employed. In this fashion, the parents would hire the teacher to teach their children.

An illustration of autonomy in the teaching profession is the case of my godmother. She was an autonomous teacher in the 1950s and 1960s. She had a one-room school in the garage of her home in the city of São Paulo, Brazil. She lived in a low- to middle-class neighborhood within a large metropolitan area, and she taught children from first to fourth grades, all together in one classroom. In those days in Brazil, school was not compulsory, and very few were funded by the government. Most schools were private, and elementary education ended in the fourth grade. If successful, the student received an elementary education diploma and was ready to enter the *ginasio*, equivalent to our middle school of today. My godmother taught the neighborhood children and successfully prepared them to enter the *ginasio*.

Within any academic year, her one-room school served anywhere from 15 to 30 students at different grade levels. This is how she made a living, and she was successful. In fact, toward the latter part of her career, she was teaching the children and grandchildren of the first students she had at the early part of her career. Local neighborhood families were happy to pay her to educate their children. She taught the appropriate curriculum so her students were successful when entering the next level, and she did what was necessary to make her school valid in the city and the state. However, she was her own boss, and she made all decisions about what and how her students learned. She truly had autonomy.

Conversely, as public employees, teachers could not function with a similar level of autonomy. Within our nation's school system, teachers have to be accountable for the content of instruction so that there is coherence in the bodies of knowledge taught to students within our society. Nevertheless, as expert professionals of pedagogy, they should also be given the space to make the appropriate decisions in their classrooms to promote the best learning. This would include teaching the agreed-upon content and more.

In other words, they should have the knowledge of what to teach and cover this content as expected. However, they should also have the knowledge and skill to teach effectively and the freedom to decide which approaches to use and when to use them. This I call "teacher agency," for it defines a freedom to act within the structures of the professional space.

## AGENCY WITHIN THE SCHOOL STRUCTURE

Agency in relation to structure is a topic more familiar to sociologists and organizational theorists than educators in general. The agency/structure paradigm has been debated by sociologists and philosophers for a long time. Reed (2003) defines *agency/structure* as a dilemma that has preoccupied organizational theorists for more than two decades, leading to four different philosophical approaches that position agency and structure in different relationships to each other. All examine the relationships between an individual's ability to act with agency and the social or organizational structures that may constrain such acts. Within educational systems, such as public schools, it makes a great deal of sense to examine teacher agency through this sociological perspective to get a better understanding of how it can flourish.

Among the four approaches to the debate, the *reductionist* approach seems to be the model that is assumed by policy makers, perhaps unwittingly. In this behaviorist approach, the world consists of individuals driven by self-interests of material or biological nature, not by intersubjective considerations. In other words, individuals are not driven by ethical or moral values or the desire to do good for society. Therefore, organizational leaders work so that "individual behavior is . . . driven by standardized operational procedures based on rules of rational calculation" (Reed, 2003, p. 292). Within school systems, operational procedures translate to school calendars, curriculum, standardized tests, and all other school processes driven by policies and mandates.

The reductionist approach echoes of teacher evaluations and the monetary rewards offered to those teachers whose students pass standardized tests. It also reminds us of the reasoning behind the continuous supervision of teachers to maintain their teaching acts within the limits of the prescribed practices. This top-down approach assumes a linear means-ends rationality that disregards the messiness of human experience, such as social and cultural contexts, learning abilities, individuality, and identity.

A more drastic approach that minimizes the value of agency even further than reductionism is called *determinism*. In this approach, agency is practically nonexistent, and social structures are the long-lasting forces that pervade all beings. In *determinism* the "only agent of social action is structure itself" (Walsh, 1998, p. 11), with systems being the major regulators of individuals' actions.

Another approach, *relationism/realism*, contends that agency and structure are interdependent. The creativity and constraint present in the dilemma should be recognized as constitutive features of social and organizational structures (Reed, 2003). Some say that in relationism/realism the focus on structure is at the expense of the concept of self (Trigg, 2001, p. 252). It seems to be favored by organizational theorists who are more interested in developing structures than in creating spaces for individual agency.

A final way of examining the dilemma of agency/structure presented by Reed (2003) is called *conflationism*. It is founded on "constructivist ontology . . . (focusing) on analysis of social practices and the creation of institutional structures by social actors" (Reed, 2003, p. 3). As such, the conflationist approach is most analogous with sociocultural theory, also referred to as cultural-historic psychology, which was first developed by Vygotsky and a circle of researchers in the Soviet Union during the early part of the last century (Yasnitsky, Veer, and Ferrari, 2014).

Agency in the sociocultural framework positions individuals' actions as always being shaped by the social norms surrounding those acts. Even when the individual's actions are aimed at resisting or rebelling against the social and cultural norms, those actions have a purpose within the context of where they occur. Furthermore, the study of individuals' actions or ways of being can only be analyzed as centered within a social system. Yet, it does not extinguish the importance of the individual. Rather, it provides the means for studying human development within the social world we live in. That is, agents always can and do make choices, but their choices are both enabled and constrained by who they are and their situation at the time of the choice.

Our choices, of course, are crucial to both who we are and the situations we find ourselves in. This seems to be the most fitting sociological approach to understanding agency within the structure of school systems. Utilizing a conflationist approach, we can examine the teacher as an agent and the school system as the structure where the teacher functions professionally.

For the purposes of fostering and studying teacher agency within the structures of school systems, I define teacher agency as a teacher's capacity to make professional choices based on the knowledge and expertise of ways to produce learning and development in students. Although some teacher educators reject the sociological view of agency altogether, I believe it is important to consider various disciplines to fully develop the construct.

The sociological perspective includes the importance of the context, or structures where an individual can exercise agency. Priestley, Biesta, and Robinson (2015) have a well-developed understanding of agency, calling it the ecological approach. This definition of *agency* sees it as an achievement, not a personal capacity. Agency requires that individuals act by appropriating the resources within their environment. Therefore, the achievement of agency requires the interplay between the individual efforts, the available resources, and contextual and structural factors acting on unique situations (Biesta and Tedder, 2007).

Applying this definition to the context of the teaching profession, the concept of teacher agency presented here requires at the onset two assumptions of teaching:

1. *A public view of teaching as a valued, complex profession.*
   Conceptualizing teaching as a complex and highly specialized profession is not the view currently held by many, who believe that almost anyone can teach. Most do not realize that it requires specialized pedagogical knowledge and the ability to apply it in varied situations and contexts for the benefit of the students' holistic development. This holistic development refers to the fact that a teacher's task is not only to impart knowledge of academic subjects but also to facilitate the cognitive, emotional, and physical development of students. Certainly with this understanding of the complexities of the teaching profession, policy makers would be more careful in designing educational policies to seek the advice of teachers and educators with many years of expertise.
2. *A teacher's authoritative confidence and awareness of preparedness.*
   The second prerequisite to the existence of teacher agency is authoritative self-confidence. In this case, teachers would feel proud of their occupation rather than apologetic. How often have we heard the phrase "You're just a teacher?" or "What is taught in the college of education is not a discipline." These kinds of comments undervalue the teaching profession, leading teachers to hold low expectations of themselves. Often this promotes passivity, and they expect directions about what to do and when.

Under the right conditions, teachers know they have the right and obligation to make professional decisions so their students learn. Being a complex profession, teaching also requires that teachers engage in critical reflections about their professional actions and in inquiry-based dialogue to further the development of their practices and of the profession. Under the right conditions, not only are they willing to engage fully, but they are also confident of their capacity to fulfill their professional duties successfully.

Therefore, teacher agency requires a sociocultural context where teaching is valued and the teacher derives from public opinion a sense of assuredness in the capacity to act professionally through informed choices. Of course, this requires teacher-preparation programs that are appropriately developed with all of the components that ensure the abilities of their graduates. The work presented in this book examines teacher agency within an agency/structure perspective most in harmony with the conflationist sociological perspective and the sociocultural approach to human development.

Chapter 1 presents a detailed explanation of teacher agency, followed by a sociohistorical analysis of teacher agency in chapter 2, with an emphasis on how it has been lost across time due to educational policies and sociopolitical trends in the United States. This chapter also explains how the presence of teacher agency is crucial to school improvement, increased job satisfaction, and decreased teacher attrition. Part I culminates in chapter 3, which presents a theoretical framework based on *adult learning theory*, *cultural historical theory*, and *critical pedagogy*, with the goal of promoting the development of teacher agency as an integral part of the teacher archetype; in other words, making it a part of the individual teacher identity and society's view of the profession.

While the emphasis of part I is theoretical, part II focuses on how teacher agency functions in practice. It draws attention to the application of the principles presented in part I by first examining one teacher who was able to exercise agency within the structure of a school system. Chapter 4, which is authored by teacher Lileana Ríos-Ledezma, presents an analysis of her five-year journey in a self-study format. She explains her perspectives on teacher agency.

Chapter 5 analyzes the elements present in the school structure that allowed this teacher to exercise agency successfully and suggests other examples of teachers' practices for the promotion of teacher agency. Most importantly, this chapter can be a most appropriate reading for the teachers themselves. It presents specific principles that can be applied in the classroom, even in settings where teacher agency is not customarily considered. Chapter 6 concludes the book with a discussion of the kinds of support school administrators and teacher educators can provide to promote teacher agency.

*Part I*

# Agency in the Teaching Profession

"I hadn't really thought about how prescribed everything I was doing at Craig [High School] was. I had to use the prescribed book list, in the prescribed order, at the prescribed page, using a prescribed budget. There was so little opportunity to tailor what I was doing for the individual students I was working with, whether they were far beyond or far behind. I couldn't hook them on literature by first handing them a book that reflects their interests."—Farris-Berg, Dirkswager, and Junge, 2012, p. 5

In most instances, teachers are not aware of the limitations placed on them, as evident in this quote. Though teachers often are quite adept at knowing how to make their teaching more meaningful for their students, they are not afforded the space to do so. In this section of the book, teacher agency is presented from a theoretical and historical perspective. The ultimate goal is to understand why it is not an integral part of the profession and what can be done to promote it.

The term is defined in detail in chapter 1, along with an explanation of why it should be an integral part of the teaching profession. Then, chapter 2 presents a historical account of teaching in the United States and why professional agency has not been a central element of teaching. Chapter 3, the final chapter in this section, focuses on a set of theoretical principles for the development of teachers who can exercise agency as professionals based on critical pedagogy, sociocultural learning theory, and adult learning principles. This theoretical framework is aimed at fostering the development of teachers who make decisions based on their knowledge, expertise, and a vision of education as an integral part of our democracy.

*Chapter One*

# What Is Teacher Agency?

> "In our rush to reform education, we have forgotten a simple truth: reform will never be achieved by renewing appropriations, restructuring schools, rewriting curricula, and revising texts if we continue to demean and dishearten the human resource called the teacher on whom much depends. . . . [N]one will transform education if we fail to cherish and challenge the human heart that is the source of good teaching."—Parker Palmer, 2007, p. 4

Although the interest in teacher agency is becoming more prevalent in education literature, it is still an emerging concept. Some closely related terms encountered in the literature are *teacher autonomy* and *teacher leadership*. The three terms—*teacher agency, teacher autonomy,* and *teacher leadership*—are not synonymous. The inadequacy of the term *teacher autonomy* as an element of the profession is explained in the introduction. Essentially, *autonomy* implies a level of independence not present in educational structures.

*Teacher leadership*, on the other hand, is also not sufficient because it is recognized by a set of skills not present in all teachers and not an integral part of the teaching profession. The implication is that some teachers have the capacity to be leaders, while others do not. However, *teacher agency* as defined is considered an integral part of the teaching identity and recognized as a key element of the profession, even though currently this is not fully recognized.

The accountability environment of education in the United States has focused on improving the quality of educational outcomes based on a set of assumptions about teaching and what takes place within the classroom. In fact, much of the dialogue about accountability and the evils of education has focused on the excessive use of testing, the dumbing-down of the curriculum (Ravitch, 2010), and the need for equitable funding and resources to schools

(Arce et al., 2010). However, the teacher has been left out of the dialogue, as highlighted by Parker Palmer (2007) at the start of this chapter, first published in 1998. It is sad to see that the statement is still true, twenty years after it was originally made.

## WHY TEACHER AGENCY?

Some may argue that there is no value to teacher agency and that it is best to leave school structure the way it is. For them, teacher agency may be ludicrous because teachers are not ready for decision making. Perhaps this view is the fear of what may result from teachers having the freedom to act with agency. Usually, it is school leaders who question the possibility of allowing teachers to decide the best course of action in their daily practices because it may hurt their own positions. "Why should we not allow teachers to function as technicians?" they may ask. While others may add, "Why not let teachers be the ones to carry out the job of teaching their students and let the curricular decisions be made by the school and district administrators?" In their opinions, this is good advice because administrators usually have more years of experience in the educational field. In addition, educational administrators are seen as more aware of the organizational aspects of school systems, as they have an additional educational preparation. To become school leaders, they have undergone specialized certification processes that allow them to exercise their positions as curriculum developers, school principals, and superintendents.

The most reasonable argument for reconsidering the status quo and seeking to reframe the teaching profession is that the educational system as it is currently functioning is faulty. This is evident by the low performance of our students when compared to other nations. One well-respected source of evidence for this fact comes from the Programme for International Students Assessment (PISA), developed by the Organisation for Economic Co-operation and Development (OECD). This triennial test is given to more than a half-million fifteen-year-olds in seventy-two nations. The two-hour test evaluates different kinds of knowledge and skills, including mathematics, reading, and science (OECD, 2016). In the last test, administered in 2015, Singapore ranked number 1, followed by Japan and Estonia. Finland, a country that had ranked number 1 in the past and recognized as a model, placed number 5 in the most recent report, which still ranks them among the top ten countries in the world.

The United States was ranked number 25 on the list. Obviously, there is no reason to maintain the current educational structure. As evidenced in these results, we are not faring well in our task of educating our nation's children. It seems we are not preparing them to reach their potential to contribute to our society. Therefore, we must seek to transform our system to one that is more appropriate and beneficial.

Historically, policy makers have focused their attention on accountability measures to improve our educational system. While accountability and curriculum are important areas of concern, the discussion about them should include all professionals engaged in the education process. Yet the teachers' perspective is missing in the dialogue, despite their knowledge and expertise, because they are blamed for our failure to improve education outcomes.

We can interpret from educational policies that teachers are blamed for our students not being as academically ready as those in other nations. For example, the NCLB policies pressured all schools to have all students reach proficiency, as defined by each state. The effect of this policy is well documented; teacher autonomy decreased, and the curriculum became prescriptive (Center for Education Policy, 2008).

The allocation of instruction time was narrowed toward tested subjects (Dee and Jacob, 2010), and teachers' evaluations are in part based on their students' test results, with the use of a value-added concept (Braun, 2005). Though NCLB has been supplanted by the Every Student Succeeds Act (ESSA) in 2015, it will take some time before the system is reformed, and we cannot yet envision a system that will include the teachers' perspectives in designing the solutions for an improved education for all students.

We can surmise from the policies and their implementation that the purpose of accountability is to make schools and teachers accountable for their professional actions. So, the assumption is that punitive measures will lead to better-quality instruction. Another assumption detected in the educational policy debates is that the lack of positive results in learning is caused by a lack of appropriate preparation. To solve this problem, monies are spent on new and improved professional development to increase the teachers' abilities to teach.

## WHERE ARE THE TEACHERS' PERSPECTIVES?

Although the quality of instruction or the preparation of the teaching force are logical explanations for the outcomes of standardized tests, why are teachers not included in the dialogues about solutions to our educational problems? After all, the role of teachers should be a crucial element in the dialogue, for they are the professionals who are, in fact, in the best position to understand the learning process and the obstacles that prevent its unfolding. They should be included as equal collaborators in the discussion, for they can bring insightful perspectives to promote better results.

In other words, the discussions about curriculum, methods, and ways to measure the results need to include the perspectives of those in the front line, and their voices should be valued for the professional perspectives they bring to the dialogue. After all, when traditionally certified, a teacher has gone through the appropriate training to become a professional and at least has, at the onset of their careers, some expertise about how to lead the classroom activities in ways that will not only promote learning but also advance the overall development of their students. With appropriate professional development and after a few years of experience, this expertise increases, and the teacher can be quite effective, if given the space to make professional decisions in the classroom. With daily face-to-face contact with their students, teachers' perspectives on the ways to improve education should be of the utmost importance.

There may be some criticisms about the preparation of teachers, especially if they have undergone alternative means to certification. Though many alternatively certified teachers eventually become excellent educators, unfortunately, they are not fully prepared when they first enter their teaching careers. They lack the pedagogical knowledge acquired through coursework and field-based experiences included in regular university-based certification programs. Nevertheless, if they are trusted with the education of our nation's children, once they have completed the certification process and acquired the pedagogical expertise through experience, they, too, should be valued as professionals and their perspectives included in the educational dialogue. Yet, though prepared for their careers, teachers are rarely given the chance to make the appropriate choices that are specific to the context of their classrooms and the needs of their students, and they are never given the opportunity to contribute to the national dialogue about educational reform.

In addition to not being a part of the dialogue of possible solutions, teachers are stripped of their right to act in ways that can lead to better outcomes. Indeed, today, most teachers have no agency in how they teach, especially in schools that serve populations of so-called at-risk students. In these schools, teachers are generally treated as robots who must repeat the script provided in the curriculum manuals given to them by their supervisors.

When teachers are inundated with an overabundance of techniques, they cease to think critically about their practices or to reflect about the ways to improve outcomes. The techniques mandated, though appropriate in some instances, lose their effectiveness when combined in incoherent ways. The result is that teachers mindlessly apply the smorgasbord of techniques imposed on them by their supervisors, too afraid to diverge to other approaches they know may be more appropriate in case they get caught. The consequence for diverging from the mandated curriculum may be a poor evaluation or, worse, the loss of their jobs. This is especially problematic in right-to-work states, where teachers are not protected by a professional union.

Obviously, what is proposed in this book is quite different from the current condition of the teaching profession, for it lacks teacher agency as an integral part. In order to fully understand this concept, it is important to define teacher agency within the context of professionalism.

## TEACHING AS A PROFESSION

Some people question the idea that teaching is a profession; others argue that profession as a concept is an outdated idea. For example, according to Taylor and Runté (1995), the concept of a profession is founded on two outdated sociological theories, namely the *trait model* and *structural functionalism*. The trait model of professionalism is based on sets of traits, or specialized knowledge, that specific professionals have, which are questioned for their validity.

As explained by Taylor and Runté (1995), another outdated sociological theory applied to the promotion of teaching as a profession is called *structural-functional theory*, which seeks to connect theories to traits. Through the application of this sociological theory, professional organizations who oversee the standards for a profession develop competency-based assessments or processes to validate the profession and to attest that candidates who meet their standards have attained the necessary level of knowledge to consider themselves members of the profession. Examples of this approach are the American Medical Association (AMA) and the National Conference of Bar Examiners (NCBE).

Applying the principles of structural functionalism to teaching leads to an understanding that teaching is not a profession because, for teachers, the gatekeepers of the profession are not educators but special bodies inside each state government. These governmental institutions oversee the teacher-certification process for each state in the United States, and its members are not necessarily educators, which is a general prerequisite for the members of other organizations that set professional standards, such as the AMA and the NCBE. Nevertheless, sociologists have generally abandoned these theories because traits are, for the most part, arbitrary, undefined, and lacking clear standards. Hence, trait models and structural functionalism are based on ideology.

We can attest to the presence of these identified weaknesses in applying these models to the teaching profession. For example, the standards for becoming a teacher vary greatly from state to state and even from program to program. One can become a teacher through university-based programs or alternative certification paths. The variations in the preparation process are numerous, not only between these two types of certifications, but also within each type. The only standard in the certification process within each state is based on the certification exams to assess the knowledge of specific traits agreed upon by the state's education policy-making body in the field, which is made up of people who do not possess knowledge of pedagogy, curriculum, or human development.

If we examine the certification exams for each state, we see that there are some general similarities between the types of knowledge assessed in these exams, such as content knowledge, pedagogical knowledge, and pedagogical content knowledge. However, when analyzing the details in the traits expected of a teacher, undoubtedly, we see variations in the specific kinds of knowledge that are valued by each of the states' certification agencies.

Likewise, there are enormous variances in the kinds of skills that must be demonstrated beyond passing certification exams. For example, in addition to demonstrating their knowledge on a theoretical level, future teachers need to demonstrate how they apply their knowledge in real classrooms, so they are also evaluated through observations of their teaching in real classroom settings. These evaluations make use of observational protocols based on specific traits they must demonstrate, and these evaluation tools also vary widely across states and certification programs.

After certification and employment in a school, teachers receive continuous evaluations based on varying assessment instruments, which often have no real research to support their validity. There have been attempts to organize the standards into a national system, such as those developed by the National Board of Professional Teaching Standards (NBPTS). However, this national standard is not obligatory, nor is it applicable at the initial stage of the teaching career because teachers must have some experience before attempting this higher level of certification. Therefore, applying the trait model to the teaching profession is problematic because educators have not yet been successful in reaching a consensus on the set of mandatory traits for teachers. Nor have teacher educators been recognized as the appropriate people to create the standards for certification.

Taylor and Runté (1995) explain that these kinds of processes are intended to promote codes of ethics and self-regulation through associations designed to restrain professionals from engaging in practices that take unfair advantage of the specialized knowledge they possess. Upon close analysis, we can see that the development of procedures for professionalization is based on the assumption that structures for the profession are instituted to protect the public from a monopoly of knowledge.

In their book, Taylor and Runté (1995) give a clear explanation of issues surrounding the professionalization of teaching from a sociological perspective, arguing against its status as a profession. Yet, educators still recognize that society, at large, accepts some occupations as professions based on a consensus about their value and the required expert preparation (Musingafi and Chiwanza, 2014). Therefore, educators regard teaching as a profession because it requires specialized knowledge and ethics, and because teachers as professionals, like lawyers and medical doctors, are held accountable for the work they perform.

While the professionalization of teaching is advocated for, comparisons to the medical profession are frequently made. This is due to the many similarities between these two professions. Both the medical doctor and the teacher must have adequate preparation to exercise their practices appropriately, though this fact is not always recognized for the teaching profession, which must be remediated if we are to succeed in achieving optimal education for our citizens.

Also, like medical doctors, a teacher's work is complex and based on decisions that do not always lead to the same positive results. Like doctors, teachers are in a profession that requires ethical values, for their decisions undoubtedly have a significant impact on the lives of the human beings who are in their care. Yet, though the status of the medical profession is somewhat diminished in the current environment of health care policies in the government, it is nevertheless still regarded as more prestigious than teaching.

Even though teaching may be considered a profession by some, it is not valued or adequately supported by the public. As explained in the introduction, the frequent bad publicity presented through the media leads to the current devaluing of the profession, which prevents teachers from exercising their right to apply their knowledge in the classroom in order to lead their students to achieve their potential. Therefore, it is imperative that educators at all levels work to remedy these situations and transform the public views of teaching to one that sees it for what it is.

As we consider teaching a profession, the decisions and policies about education must include the educators at the forefront. This means that all types of educators should be in charge of decision making in education matters, especially teachers. All policies about curriculum, preparation, certification, and evaluation should be created and overseen by educational professionals, especially those who work in the classroom, in order to create the structures necessary to make teacher agency possible.

## TEACHING AS THE ACT OF BUILDING BRIDGES

Another dilemma in understanding the nature of teaching lies in conceptualizing it as an art or a science. Currently, teaching as a science seems to be the most accepted view. It is most evident in the U.S. Department of Education and its Institute of Educational Sciences. Through these agencies' patterns of funding for educational research, ideologically they view teaching as a science.

Funding of research is limited to studies that are quantitative and make use of experimental or quasi-experimental models. The impetus is on viewing education, or learning in particular, as the result of cognition and the functions of the brain. While this approach is valuable, learning is too complex to be limited to these types of studies. Human development is made up of integrated and interrelated processes that include not only cognition but also physical and emotional processes of equal importance in the lives of humans from diverse racial, ethnic, cultural, and linguistic groups, who coexist in social spaces that are ever intermingling and expanding.

The lens used by positivistic, scientifically based, quantitative studies is limited in its capacity to elucidate the intricacies of human development within complex societies. Furthermore, the specific perspective used by scientists who view humans as purely biological beings is biased and oversimplified. Their perspective leads to the reduction of teaching to tidbits of unconnected knowledge and overlooks the ways and means of interconnecting the knowledge or connecting it to the learners and their diverse identities.

The scientific approach is also based on assumptions about the value of what is measured. In other words, why are specific questions used in school assessments? Who decides what is important? Why is it important? Is the assessed knowledge important to all? Why? What about assessing the ways that knowledge can be used? Or, how can we be open to the possibility that our means are incorrect? What happens when all learners are successful in acquiring the knowledge valued by those in power to make these decisions? Will there still be room for differences of opinion or diversity in values, culture, language, or identities? How? Thinking about the answers to these questions may help us realize the level of complexity present in learning and our purposes for education.

We can also look at teaching as an art. We may think of the teaching act as architecture, for example. Architecture is the design, planning, and construction of a physical structure. In the process, the architect applies scientific principles so that the product is sturdy, durable, and practical. But the architect also takes into consideration the contextual factors, such as the type of terrain where the structure will be built, the proper materials for its strength and durability, and the social-cultural context of where it will be located. Who will use it and why? Finally, the architect also considers the aesthetic value given to the structure by its users and its artist, the architect.

When building complex structures, such as tall buildings or bridges, the architect needs to work with an engineer, who has a deeper understanding of the limitations and capabilities of the materials being used or the scientific knowledge necessary to ensure its stability. So, in essence, both science and art are integral parts of building structures. We want structures that are strong and safe, but we also want them to have an aesthetic value.

Similarly, the act of teaching and learning is the process of facilitating the development of the human capacity; it is much like the building of a bridge. In this metaphor, the teacher is the architect who must connect the knowledge to the learner. This is done through the act of teaching, where the teacher must apply the principles of the cognitive sciences and human development.

Teaching requires the application of the current knowledge of how learning occurs. However, teaching must also be an aesthetic act that considers the social and cultural aspects of the classroom where learning is occurring. It considers the identities of the teacher and the learners. When the learning process is more complex, such as in the case of teaching students with disabilities, then the teacher must work with a specialist, much like the architect who works with the engineer in the building of more-complex structures.

In this debate, the most crucial aspect to keep in mind is that teachers are charged with preparing our nation's children to become adept citizens and well-rounded individuals who can contribute to our society in a well-balanced way. It is too limiting to think of teachers as solely responsible for the cognitive and academic development of students because well-balanced human beings rely on a concerted functioning of the different aspects of their beings. Namely, the physical, socioemotional, and cognitive aspects must work together. Thus, teaching is a highly complex endeavor requiring knowledge, expertise, and a specific set of dispositions.

The multifaceted development of students cannot be expected to occur as the result of a merely technical approach. The teacher cannot blindly follow the demands of a supervisor who is not in direct contact with the students. Furthermore, the supervisor's expertise often does not match the expertise of the teacher; therefore, the supervisor is not as knowledgeable of the nuances of the teaching-learning act. This happens because often the principal's or other school administrator's area of certification is different from that required of the teachers. For example, the principal in an elementary school may hold an initial certification in a content area for high school teaching and has no knowledge of how to teach elementary school children in general classrooms or special and bilingual education classes.

Therefore, principals do not always have the adequate experience to understand the ramifications of specific approaches to instruction within the varied contexts of each classroom in their schools. In the school structure, their primary goal is the management of the school based on governmental demands made at the local, state, and federal levels. Because students are not robots who function appropriately given the right programming and humans are diverse and complex, teaching should be in the hands of an adept, knowledgeable professional—the teacher. A crucial aspect of being a professional is the ability to make professional decisions; in other words, to exercise agency.

## AGENCY IS PART OF THE TEACHING PROFESSION

What is proposed here is not new but has been stated by other educators who have realized that, for educational renewal to be effective, it needs to value the role of the teacher as a central figure in the process (Cohn, 1992; Farris-Berg, Dirkswager, and Junge, 2012; Shohamy, 2009; Villegas-Reimers and Reimers, 1996). In particular, Villegas-Reimers and Reimers have voiced their concerns over the lack of teachers' voices in the process of selection, training, and supervision of teachers on a global scale.

Throughout the world, reform has excluded the teacher as an integral part of the process for school renewal. The exclusion takes many forms, ranging from "'teacher-proof' innovations, which can sustain the impetus for change in spite of the teachers" (Villegas-Reimers and Reimers, 1996, p. 469) to simply not including their perspectives in the discourse about reforms. The archetype of teaching as profession presented here is, therefore, innovative and requires a new vision for teacher preparation and educational policy making. Central aspects of teacher preparation include the recruitment of highly capable individuals into the teaching profession and after professional preparation, giving teachers a central role in the dialogue about school reform and policies.

*Chapter Two*

# A Sociohistorical Look at the Loss of Teacher Agency

"I quit because I can't stand seeing kids come to class hungry and needing shoes. I thought I could do more by organizing farm workers than by trying to teach their hungry children."—Dolores Huerta

Activist Dolores Huerta, who organized migrant farm workers in the 1960s, was a former teacher. Her activism was the result of her choice to leave the profession because she felt she could do more by promoting change outside the classroom, as expressed in this quote. This was clearly an act of agency on the part of a teacher.

Questions emerge from the statement made by this teacher/activist:

1. Does agency always have to take place outside the classroom?
2. Is there a way for teachers to be an integral part of positive societal change choosing to teach?
3. Was there ever a time when teachers could exercise agency while practicing the occupation we call teaching?
4. Across history, what kinds of acts did teachers perform with agency, such as making decisions based on their knowledge and expertise?

## THE HISTORICAL BEGINNING OF TEACHING IN THE UNITED STATES

To answer these questions, one must examine the status of teaching as a profession across time. In the United States, teaching was often considered a temporary job. For example, in early colonial and postcolonial times, teaching was not really considered a permanent occupation but a temporary means of earning a living until an individual could transition into a more permanent position. In rural areas, it was performed mostly by men who had other occupations, like farming, for example.

Farmers taught during the off season, when the crops had already been harvested and it was not yet time to sow the new crops. Those who were more ambitious and educated became teachers temporarily and then they moved on to study in preparation for a new occupation of higher status, usually in church or law. Also, until the early nineteenth century, it was easy to consider teaching a temporary job, for it did not require any special training but only a good moral character; the ability to read, write, and do arithmetic; and, in some cases, knowledge of Latin (Levin, 2000).

Generally, in this early phase of our nation's development, there was a value for learning to read, especially because this was considered an important skill for those of religious upbringing. Learning to read was the best way to learn about God's teachings in the Bible, so it was often promoted by churches and religious organizations. However, schools were not plentiful and certainly not systematized because education was not compulsory.

Many of the early schools were housed in the homes of literate women and were called dame schools. The curriculum in these schools varied greatly, but literacy was expected for all children, no matter the social class. In dame schools, women teachers taught the very young to read and write. Then some boys moved on to other schools to prepare them for higher education, while most girls continued their education at home, where they learned cooking, sewing, and homemaking. Usually, they were taught by their mothers. In larger communities, schooling was provided at a schoolhouse by a schoolmaster, who was always an educated man.

We can infer, then, that teaching was not really considered a profession, for it did not require a formal set of processes to enter the occupation, nor was it considered a permanent occupation. Yet, because of its lack of formality, one can assume that there was some level of agency, for teachers chose what and how to teach according to their best judgment. In dame schools, women were free to act according to what they thought was best, even though they were limited by what society expected of them. Indeed, we can deduce that most women generally would not challenge the status quo and that the education of the girls they taught ended as soon as the young girls could read enough to understand the "holy book."

Until the 1830s, schools were private institutions, so schooling was not affordable to all individuals. Public schooling came into being as the result of the work of Horace Mann. He was not a teacher or an educator but a legislator, nominated for the position of secretary of the State Board of Education in Massachusetts at its inception. He was later elected to the U.S. House of Representatives. Mann proposed a school system that would be free and nonsectarian, available to all, regardless of their social class, and mostly funded by taxes (Cubberley, 1947). In this manner, Mann promoted the creation of the common schools, a precursor to today's public schools. He believed education should be provided by the government for its people, with the aim of benefiting society by preparing its citizens.

With the advent of the common school through Mann's ideas, the teaching profession grew exponentially in a relatively short time. These schools, first opened in Massachusetts, were then emulated in other regions and states, with the idea of educating all of our nation's children and preparing them to become productive citizens in a democratic society. As the idea took hold and new schools began sprouting across the nation, there was an increased need for teachers. This led to the period in public education referred to as the period of feminization of the teaching profession (Levin, 2000).

The 1840s is the decade recognized as the era when women were first formally welcomed into the teaching occupation. It is saddening to note that, though women were given the opportunity to enter the workforce, they were paid much less than their male counterparts. Proponents who encouraged this idea argued that women were naturally suited for teaching but for a third of the cost.

Yet, though poorly paid, women welcomed the idea of becoming teachers. They often had no interest in a long-term commitment for the position. They considered it a good opportunity for earning some money, but only until they got married, when holding a job outside of the home would no longer be considered an option. Until the time of World War II, most married women were not allowed to teach either by law or policy. Also, for many women, teaching was a more attractive option for work than other occupations available to them at the time, which included factory work, housekeeping, nursing, and clerical work.

These women teachers experienced agency precisely because they did not really depend on their occupation for survival or as a path to higher positions. They also derived a sense of purpose and public usefulness from their positions. As teachers, they made decisions in their classrooms and about the professional development activities they would engage in. They attended summer trainings and formed associations where they networked and exchanged ideas. In many ways, they promoted change in their communities (Levin, 2000). Some of them truly affected society in different ways, as they advocated for transformations that promoted social justice.

The following women were change agents in the early days, when women played crucial roles in the development of teaching as a profession:

- Catherine Beecher, a self-educated woman, wrote many essays that advocated for the important role women played in education and cofounded the Hartford Female Seminary, a school that trained women to be mothers and teachers (Hoffman, 2003).

- Charlotte Forten was another leader in the education of children. She was an African American woman from Philadelphia who chose to move south to teach the children of freed slaves (Hoffman, 2003).
- Emma Hart Willard devoted her life to advocating for women's rights to intellectual equality (Hoffman, 2003).

The list goes on; there are many women who took advantage of their status as teachers to exercise agency and become agents of change.

Indeed, these women are notable. We must recognize that, in subtle and perhaps not so subtle ways, these teachers found ways to exercise agency within their occupational space despite the growing oppression within the profession precisely because most of them were women. Nevertheless, the level of teacher agency decreased as schools grew into public systems, where men were the administrators supervising the women teachers. With consolidation and as schools grew in size and numbers, there was a need to structure them as organizations for learning. A principal headed these schools, and groups of schools within towns and cities were led by a superintendent. These administrators were mostly men, who would pressure the great numbers of teachers to improve the quality of their work (Hoffman, 2003).

## AGENCY IN THE FORM OF MILITANCY

In the United States, teacher agency came as a result of actively fighting for a cause. Teachers fought for the improvement of conditions in schools that were detrimental to them as teachers, as well as to the students they taught. Such is the case of the birth of teacher unions toward the end of the nineteenth century. From the 1890s to 1910, transformation in education came as the result of militancy. It is important to consider that activism permeated through this era, not only in education, but also in civil rights in general.

The activism present at that time was led by those who fought for the rights of the socially victimized. This was the era when African Americans, Native Americans, and women were the focal points of political debate because they did not hold equal rights in society. Among the famous activists of this time are Susan B. Anthony, who fought for women's right to vote; Elaine Goodale Eastman, who fought for the rights of Native American children in schools; Frederick Douglass, who fought for the rights of African Americans; and Margaret Haley, the creator of the Chicago Teachers Federation, which later became the American Federation of Teachers, as it consolidated the various teacher unions that followed (Goldstein, 2015; Levin, 2000).

By the end of the nineteenth century, three-quarters of the teaching workforce were women receiving half as much as their male counterparts (Goldstein, 2015). Indeed, their salaries, frozen for thirty years, were often lower than that of laborers. There was also a lack of benefits or job security, and their work was scrutinized intensely. The country became more urbanized and more populated with the arrival of recent immigrants, who did not speak the language or who came from impoverished homes. Thus, teaching became ever more complicated, and teachers had no voice in promoting better working conditions. They were expected to teach increasing numbers of children, in classrooms that were often dark and poorly ventilated.

This was the fertile ground for the uprising of teachers and the formation of unions. Ironically, like Dolores Huerta, all of these women activists named here had once been teachers, and their impact on society did not come from their acts of agency within the classroom but in activism in the political arena.

## PROGRESSIVISM AND TEACHER AGENCY

Though teacher unions did promote more humane conditions in the classroom, progressivism contributed to a more emancipated role for the teacher as it relates to learning. Those who fought for the professionalization of teaching through the progressive movement include John Dewey at the turn of the twentieth century and, later, other proponents of progressive pedagogical approaches. These progressive thinkers formed part of the circle of teacher educators.

John Dewey, in particular, became a most influential American philosopher. He was a proponent of democracy in education and progressive ideas about the best ways to promote learning. A former high school teacher, he published many articles and books that have become an integral part of our knowledge about pedagogy and curriculum. Unfortunately, the impact of Dewey's ideas seems to be most significant only among teacher educators and less visible in the current practices of classroom instruction.

Though not specifically a proponent of teacher agency, in his view, both teachers and students need to be free to learn (Levin, 2000). His ideas are founded in a naturalistic approach to human development that saw individuals as active participants in learning and knowledge as the result of active adaptations to the environment. In other words, human agency was a key component in Dewey's philosophy of learning. Important elements in the process were the learner's formation and testing of hypotheses, which became key components in the scientific model to be applied in instruction.

We can see evidence of Dewey's thoughts in some educational approaches to teaching, such as the 5E model of instruction in the teaching of science content. In this teaching technique, teachers engage students in the learning of science concepts though exploration and inquiry. Yet, Dewey's progressive ideas are difficult to implement now that the focus is on accountability and high-stakes testing. As a political activist who supported the teacher's union movement, he argued against the rigid approaches used in schools of his time. Dewey proposed a classroom setting that incorporated democracy at all levels, with the children engaging in inquiry and experiential learning and the teacher free to design instruction to meet the needs of each child (Levin, 2000).

Progressivism evolved through time and was central in the development of curriculum and pedagogy into the 1960s and 1970s. The concept of democracy is essential in educational progressivism, but progressivism also includes a focus on learner-centered approaches, hands-on experiences, highly personalized instruction, critical thinking, and problem solving. At the heart of the learner-centered approaches is constructivism, which views the learner as constructing knowledge from experience. This view places the teacher as a facilitator of learning rather than a lecturer. These ideas promoted the development of pedagogies that embodied thematic instruction and open classroom settings with centers where students engaged in experiential forms of learning.

These progressive ideas about learning led to transformations in the design of curriculum and the organization of schools, such as the open classroom settings of the 1960s, which is very different from the regimented, linear, skills-based teaching prevalent in today's classrooms, namely because the educational aims are in sharp contrast. Progressive education aims to educate in ways where the learner actively engages in inquiry and explorations. In the progressive classroom, the teacher orchestrates the activities led by the students' curiosity, so learning varies from classroom to classroom. Students learn bodies of knowledge in an interconnected way. Although there can be some level of commonalities that focus on the content that must be covered, the result is as varied as the students themselves. Conversely, the aim of education founded on principles of accountability focuses on teaching that leads to measurable outcomes that are uniform across school settings.

Inquiry and exploration do not lend themselves easily to measurement, so they are replaced by skills-based teaching that leads to knowledge that is measurable and standardized for all but is also limited and superficial. Furthermore, there is no room for inquiry and exploration or individuality in standardized measurable curricula. Students and teachers cannot exercise agency in the acts of teaching or learning. Therefore, teachers had more agency when progressivism was a central part of learning in schools. This required teachers with a high level of professional skills, which had already become a part of the educational fabric our nation.

## AGENCY AND THE PROFESSIONALIZATION OF TEACHING

The professionalization of teaching began with the advent of the normal schools in 1840s. As the number of schools increased drastically, so did the number of teachers in the workforce. Thus, there was a need to establish special procedures for the training of teachers in order to ensure that the quality of instruction was based on a sound curriculum and depth of knowledge. In great part, the need to create high-quality training for teachers came from the evolution of unregulated schoolhouses where young children learned to read, write, and do arithmetic to formal educational settings designed to prepare children for a life that was increasingly becoming more complex. This led to the creation of normal schools, which were specifically designed to prepare teachers. These schools really established the norms for the teaching profession, hence the name *normal school*.

Though short lived, the normal school did elevate the professionalization of teaching. Yet as the need to reach higher levels of rigor in education surfaced, there was a steady movement toward the university as the appropriate place to provide adequate knowledge of content and pedagogy. Then at the turn of the twentieth century, educational reformers began promoting the idea of the professionalization of teaching to a new level. Eventually normal schools died, and teacher preparation moved entirely to university-based programs.

## THE ACCOUNTABILITY MOVEMENT

Compared to other countries where educational policies are set at the national level, in the United States, the view has been that educational policies should be the purview of the different states. The Elementary and Secondary Education Act (ESEA), created in 1965 and reauthorized every five years, became known as the No Child Left Behind (NCLB) Act in 2002. Under the leadership of President George W. Bush, the new version of the policy created a tension between federal and state governments because it gave more power to the federal government in matters related to education. This act held schools accountable for the education of all children through the use of standardized tests.

While state legislatures have been in charge of decision making with respect to teachers' certification and curriculum implementation, the federal policies within NCLB applied a great deal of pressure on state education agencies by requiring that all public schools demonstrate the success of their students through high-stakes assessments. This is based on the assumption that students' success is solely dependent on the quality of work performed by teachers. The Every Student Succeeds Act (ESSA), signed into law in

2015, is supposed to revert to the state level the responsibilities of educational policy and accountability. Yet accountability will continue to be the driving force behind all, and high-stakes accountability has been responsible for a decrease in teacher agency.

For example, although textbooks have been used in the United State for quite some time prior to NCLB, their use in elementary schools was optional, and teachers had the freedom over whether or how to use them (Pease-Alvarez and Samway, 2012). Since NCLB, however, the right to make this choice is no longer available because, under federal pressure to perform, states and districts make decisions about the curriculum materials that must be used and how they are used. In extreme cases, teachers are not only mandated to use specific textbooks but are also told what order they should follow and sometimes the exact questions and activities they must implement each week during the academic year. This places the emphasis on fidelity to specific content and teaching approaches, regardless of individual student needs.

Furthermore, there is a focus on teacher-centered approaches, whole-class instruction, teaching of skills in isolation, and the assessment of learning based solely on tests with multiple-choice questions (Nichols and Berliner, 2007). There is no room for teachers to make informed instructional decisions based on students' backgrounds, interests, needs, and strengths. Instead, teachers are viewed as compliant implementers of decisions made by policy makers and administrators who often have no understanding of how to teach the specific types of students in each classroom.

With the new ESSA regulations taking effect, state governments are in charge of curriculum and other educational practices, yet the decision-making power for educational practices in the classroom is still in the hands of legislators and administrators, not teachers. A good example of interference in the classroom from outside its walls is the recent attention to the development of Common Core Standards. This has been a major force that will undoubtedly affect the learning outcomes of all students, as it has been adopted by the majority of states in the United States. In particular, there are concerns about its impact on English language learners (Pease-Alvarez and Samway, 2012).

## TEACHER AGENCY ACROSS HISTORY

Because the possibility of teacher agency is dependent on the view of teaching as more than just a technical career, it is important to analyze its development as a profession. Certainly, it was not viewed as such given the historical events presented in this chapter. As stated earlier, aside from the sense of freedom and the space for individual agency during the feminization of teaching, it was generally considered a transitional occupation without much opportunity for status.

Today, teaching can be a more permanent position, and given the complex nature of the learning process, teachers need time to develop expertise. Yet, teachers do not always hold their positions for a long time, as evident from the concerns about the high levels of teacher attrition (Clandinin et al., 2015; Goldhaber and Cowan, 2014). Furthermore, teaching in the United States is still a grossly underpaid profession; there is a definite gap between teachers' salaries and those of other professionals with similar education levels (Walker, 2016, August). The personal perspective presented in textbox 2.1 further illuminates the complexities that exist in teaching as a profession.

### TEXTBOX 2.1.
### A PERSONAL VIEW

I became a teacher at a most opportune time, when schools of education emphasized a progressive learning philosophy and teachers were given the space to be creative in their classrooms.

Once I completed teacher preparation at a university, I chose to teach in private schools, partly because living in New York, if employed in public schools, I would be forced to become a member of the teachers' union. My beliefs, at that time, were that unions deprofessionalized teaching. Through unionization, teachers turned their attention to their rights as workers rather than the best ways to address the learning needs of their students. I saw that, through union protection, teachers fought for their rights and their working conditions, such as the number of students in the classroom, how many hours of preparation time they were given per week, how many sick days they were allowed, and so on.

In my mind, the focus on working conditions lowered the professional status of teachers to that of skilled laborers in factories. I believed teachers, as professionals, should not have the need to protect their working rights. In my mind, they were similar to doctors and lawyers and respected as professionals, so they did not need them.

I only realized how naïve I had been in my views about teacher unions after I became a teacher educator and moved to Texas, *a right to work state*, in 2003. I then realized that, under the high-accountability environment that permeates education now, teacher unions can offer a limited but much-needed protection to teachers as they labor to meet unrealistic and, in many ways, unfounded demands. Indeed, though teachers should be respected as professionals, until they are, they will need unions. Yet, I wonder, can we ever raise the respect for the teaching profession while we keep unions alive?

In a country where we consider ourselves proud promoters of freedom and democracy, it is difficult to understand why our education system is in such a predicament. It is evident that Horace Mann's vision of democratic principles in a public education that is free and accessible to all has not yet been fulfilled. Education is not simply the presence of schools but the presence of institutions that promote holistic learning and development of human beings, which include academic, social, emotional, and physical development in a coherent manner.

What we have is a public education that is neither equitable nor democratic. School funding and resources are not evenly distributed, and the quality of educational experiences varies significantly depending on the socioeconomic, racial, ethnic, and linguistic variations of the students (Biddle and Berliner, 2002). Also, the quality of teacher preparation varies depending on the programs available in different states. Augmenting these problems is the fact that teaching as a profession is not valued nor respected.

To improve the conditions in education so that it can function appropriately as a setting for learning under democratic principles, we must create a space where teachers are respected for their knowledge and are ready to engage in inquiry to seek the solutions to the learning problems that exist within their classrooms. Furthermore, teachers must be allowed decision-making power and be ready to engage in developing new ways to demonstrate learning that includes various forms of assessment, not just multiple-choice standardized tests.

This level of professionalization requires more than the knowledge of institutional structures but also includes the collaboration of professionals with various expertise. To improve education, we need educational administrators, with their expertise in management of the institutional structures we call schools. These administrators need to apply their expertise in leadership to manage the schools by focusing their attention on the administrative matters, while allowing the teachers to collaborate with them in making education work. The administrators must allow the teachers to bring their respective knowledge and expertise in content; pedagogy; human development; psychology; and social, cultural, and linguistic studies as they work with the learners in their classrooms. In this complex process, we need teachers who specialize in specific aspects of the profession to collaborate in harmonious ways with school administrators and policy makers.

In addition, schools should be in partnership with universities so that teachers are then part of collaborative teams to promote the best kinds of learning for the specific contexts of their schools and the specific needs of the learners in their classrooms. In these teams, teachers can bring their expert knowledge of learning as it occurs in their classrooms, and it is a learning that values the diversity of the students they work with.

In this manner, research can be based on everyday matters in the classrooms without an artificial separation between theory and practice. In this setting, the teachers are the professionals who are engaged in the process of teaching and making decisions within the structures of the school to promote learning and human development to the highest potential. Indeed, they can engage in practitioner research, and their practices can evolve from their actions and their expertise. As professionals with expertise in the process of teaching and learning, teachers should be allowed the agency to make professional decisions within their classroom, especially decisions about how to teach the content prescribed for the grade level or the specific subjects they are teaching.

## THE NEED FOR TRANSFORMATION

This historical look at the evolution of teaching in America reveals that a major problem lies in the fact that the teaching profession has been largely under the control of policy makers at the state and national levels, with expertise in organizational and business management. Education is in the hands of those whose professions value bureaucratic and hierarchical approaches with very little, if any, consideration of actual learning, such as what it means and how it can be promoted in conjunction with the development of our young.

In many professions, the control over certification and professional practices lies with the members of the profession. Even when some level of the authority is left with the state, decisions are largely made up by professionals in their field (Angus, 2001). However, in the teaching profession, the control over certification has largely been in the hands of state officials and state boards of education. Only briefly, during the middle of the twentieth century, was the certification process in the hands of educators, when no certification exams were required in many states. Yet, even when the certification process was the purview of the education professionals, the teaching practices were largely controlled by school administrators, the state, or national government. From the time of the implementation of the Elementary and Secondary Education Act in 1965 through its reauthorization under President Bush's administration, the control had shifted increasingly toward the federal government. Now, with the creation of ESSA, this control is the moving back toward the state level. Yet the real problem is that both state and federal departments of education are largely made up of people who are not educators and have never been teachers in the classroom.

The problem is that educators are not in control of the profession and that teachers do not have the freedom to perform their duties by applying their professional knowledge. This problem is even further aggravated by the fact that the assessment of the quality of education in our schools is based in great part on statistical measures. These measures never reach the depth and analysis necessary to address the complex problems of such intervening variables as socioeconomic factors, race and discrimination, cultural and linguistic diversity, and individual differences in students.

Furthermore, assessment of the quality of our education is solely based on limited content and simplistic multiple-choice tests that reduce education to only three content areas: English language arts, mathematics, and science. In these assessments, there is no value given to other knowledge, such as health, music, and the arts. Even social studies as a content area, though evaluated at the high school level, is rarely taught in the elementary school because it is not assessed.

The analysis presented here reveals that, in order to achieve teacher agency, there needs to be a transformation in how we view public education in relation to the its role in a democratic society, with the objective of educating its citizens so they can fully engage in the democratic process during their adult years. Based on the analysis of the historical development of teaching to its current state, there needs to be a theoretical framework to transform our conceptualization of teaching within the school structure.

However, before we can engage in such a transformation of teachers who can exercise agency in coherent collaboration with educational professionals and researchers so that the students are capable of fully engaging in our society, we need a full understanding of how to develop teachers by applying principles of adult learning and sociocultural learning theories in conjunction with critical pedagogy. This is explained in the next chapter.

*Chapter Three*

# A Theoretical Framework for Promoting Teacher Agency

"Knowing, whatever its level, is not the act by which a subject transformed into an object docilely and passively accepts the contents others give or impose on him or her. Knowledge, on the contrary, necessitates the curious presence of subjects confronted with the world. It requires their transforming action on reality. It demands a constant searching. It implies invention and reinvention."—Freire, 2013, p. 89

This clearly addresses the need for learners to be active agents in their process of acquiring new knowledge. Likewise, it draws our attention to the importance for educational leaders and teacher educators to maintain this approach so teachers, who are sometimes in the position of learners, can exercise their right to teach and make professional decisions. This chapter focuses on examining specific theoretical frameworks to help us understand teacher agency as an integral part of the teacher's professional identity.

The transformation of the teacher archetype as a professional requires a completely new vision of the teacher as a subject, a thinker, and an innovator engaged in the process of knowing, as described by Paulo Freire in the opening quote. In this chapter, we examine research on teacher development and propose a theoretical framework for the promotion of teacher agency based on three theories: *adult learning theory, cultural-historical theory*, and *critical pedagogy*.

## TEACHER AGENCY—THEORY AND RESEARCH

In our search for the understanding of human nature, it may be more efficacious to avoid subscribing to a specific disciplinary approach, such as psychological, sociological, or philosophical. Rather, a deeper understanding of human nature and development comes by examining it with multiple lenses. Just like the scientist who examines physical phenomena using lenses of different color and magnification, we may apply the different disciplinary lenses to examine agency in its many forms and characteristics to derive a more comprehensive understanding. In doing so, we may find some specific details in the concept of agency that would be missed when examined by only a single disciplinary lens or approach. For example, Biesta and Tedder (2007) present an integrative approach that combines philosophy, psychology, and sociology. They explain agency as the product of our actions when we exert control over our lives within our context.

This integrative approach (Biesta and Tedder, 2007) resonates with both adult learning and cultural-historical theories of learning. It leads us to examine which kinds of activities and which contexts are conducive to the promotion of teacher agency. Which school structures allow for decision making with the purpose of promoting learning? Or what kinds of experiences from the past can teachers draw on to make decisions in the present, given the context of their classrooms or schools? This process requires a certain inquisitive stance and an openness to reflection as explained by adult learning theorists Brookfield (2017) and Mezirow (1998).

## Teacher Agency through Adult Learning Theory

Our understanding of human development suggests that teacher agency cannot just happen by simply creating the space and allowing teachers to make professional choices. Just like the development of children, the development of adult teachers is based on a process that combines cognitive, affective, and experiential aspects. An example of an educational model that integrates these components takes place at a college in New York City founded by Puerto Ricans in 1976 and that is still growing and evolving today. Boricua College uses a unique holistic approach, where learning is facilitated through a combination of contents that aim to develop all components of the individual: the cognitive, the affective, and the physical or experiential. Its humanistic approach transforms the learner so they not only acquire content knowledge but also learn to direct their own development with the guidance of the educational facilitator (Alicea, 1990; Rogers and Freiberg, 1994; Villalba, 1990).

The model combines five ways of learning, which includes the development of cognitive, affective, and experiential aspects along with theoretical and cultural content knowledge. Students engage in a metacognitive process to develop their cognitive abilities. In addition, there is a sequence of carefully designed courses through dialogical interactions to facilitate the development of affective skills, where the students become aware of personal and professional values and learn to integrate them in coherent ways in their professional practices after graduation.

Finally, student development also includes activities that allow for the analysis and evaluation of experiential learning as it intersects with the cognitive and affective components and the theoretical and cultural knowledge acquired through coursework. The result is an empowering model that achieves social justice because it especially addresses the needs of marginalized populations and transforms them into individuals with strong professional and cultural identities who are ready to become agents of change in their communities. The personal perspective in textbox 3.1 presents the model from a lived experience.

### TEXTBOX 3.1.
### A PERSONAL VIEW

As an educator, I have always favored an interdisciplinary approach to teaching and have led students to what I see as a holistic approach to learning. Nevertheless, I really learned about the importance of holistic learning from a new perspective at the postsecondary level when I began my work as an educational facilitator at Boricua College.

There, I personally observed timid students who had been unsuccessful in other educational settings engage in critical dialogue with their professors and their peers, complete their college education, and become teachers. Because at that time the college did not offer graduate studies, after graduation, our students from the teacher-preparation program entered other universities to complete the required graduate studies and obtain a permanent New York State teacher certification. They were successful, and their readiness for graduate work was noted, as they came back elated and thankful to share their stories as graduate students in prestigious universities.

This experience allowed me to understand learning as not only a memorization of concepts and principles or their application in skillful ways but also as a transformation where content and values are integrated into a coherent epistemological foundation for the engagement in purposeful and thoughtful actions aimed at solving professional problems. The Boricua College method of instruction fully promotes agency as learners become aware of their value as individuals because the authority for learning is shared with their professors, who are educational facilitators, guiding their students in a dialogical path rather than imparting lectures in a unidirectional authoritarian manner.

We can gain much insight into the development of teacher agency from this college's nationally accredited (CAEP) teacher-preparation program founded on adult learning principles and critical pedagogy.

The teacher-preparation program at Boricua College is based on a humanistic philosophy and adult learning principles. Unlike other types of educational approaches that focus primarily on the cognitive aspects of professional development, their educational model is founded on the adult learning theory of Knowles (1988) and an adaptation of educational facilitation as developed by Rodgers and Freiberg (1994).

A psychology of learning based on adult learning theories is most appropriate in teacher education because it makes use of principles most appropriate for the development of teachers who are at the adult stage of development. Working in teacher preparation is quite different from teaching children and youth because adults come into the learning process with ready-made paradigms of the world (epistemic stances) and preformed sets of values. Yet this is not always considered in teacher-preparation or professional-development programs.

Teacher training has customarily focused on the behavioral, or mechanistic, approach, which aims to control and evaluate human behavior or specific actions that were taught during a particular training. Such approaches are founded on erroneous assumptions that fail to consider the learners' values and epistemic stances, assuming that, once the specific techniques are learned, teachers would implement them.

Research demonstrates that this method of training is not effective (Yoon et al., 2007; Bush, 1984), but the cause is misunderstood. It is assumed either that the teacher did not acquire the skills taught or that they do not wish to apply them, which leads to either more numerous trainings to ensure learning or the use of rewards and punishment to promote specific behaviors. This explains the current trend in many school systems to adopt performance-based practices, such as merit pay or pay deductions based on test scores (Long, 2017, July 17; Richmond, 2012). The assumption behind these tactics is based on the false premises that test scores are solely dependent on teachers' actions in the classroom or that teachers are not motivated to engage in appropriate professional actions unless rewarded.

Because the current methods of teacher training have not been effective, we turn to an alternative theoretical stance to propose its development. The development of teacher agency would require a transformation in both the educational context of schools and in the professional identities of the teachers, so this transformation must occur within the individual teacher through a social cognitive approach. In other words, because humans are both producers and products of social systems, learning is a journey toward more complex levels of development that need to include the ability to engage in reflective judgment (King and Kitchener, 2004; Mezirow, 1998).

To comprehend teacher agency and the need for teachers to be allowed the space for decision making, we need to think about what teacher agency can actually look like. What kinds of acts and decisions should teachers make? Why? Because we are attempting to raise the professionalism in teaching, we must think of the teacher as an expert in promoting learning, much like the medical doctor is an expert in healing.

However, there are differences in the nature of the work for these two professionals, the doctor and the teacher. Medicine is founded on scientific principles at work in biological entities. While human beings are partly biological, they are also social and psychological. Therefore, while the doctor chooses among the various scientific, research-based knowledge to decide which therapies or medicines to use with specific patients depending on their ailments, teaching is more complex.

The teacher must have the knowledge of research-based practices and also be ready to modify the practices according to such contextual factors as individual students' abilities, styles of learning, culture, language, identities, and other sociopsychological elements. Therefore, the teacher needs to have an *"inquiry stance"* (Cochran-Smith and Lytle, 2009) or be ready to engage in critical reflection and practitioner research so that decisions are not haphazard but are founded on data and logical analysis. Furthermore, the teacher must have a critical stance and be ready to question the research made by others, as well as his or her own practitioner research. Specifically, important in this work on teacher agency are two aspects of adult development:

1. the development of critical reflection and
2. the ability to transform meaning perspectives

## Critical Reflection

While reflection has been a strong component of teacher preparation and development (Schön, 1984; Brookfield, 2017; Nelson and Sadler, 2012; Zeichner and Liston, 1996), promoting this kind of thinking to its optimal level is still evolving. Optimal decision making requires that we interpret and make sense of our experiences, a process called reflection, and this has been a central part of teacher education. However, it is important to understand what is meant by *reflection* because not all types of thinking are reflective. Furthermore, the most important kind of reflection that we should seek to promote in teacher development is the ability to think critically about experiences. This critical-thinking process founded on an openness to the analyses of assumptions and presuppositions leads to new interpretations and new understandings (Mezirow, 1998).

Research on reflective thinking has demonstrated that there are different kinds of reflection and different kinds of orientations in these reflections (Nelson and Sadler, 2012). There are reflections about the best techniques for approaches to teaching (technical reflection), reflections about one's own practical knowledge, specific decisions to be made based on analysis of various sources, and analyses that examine one's own assumptions of which practices promote inequities (critical reflection).

These different types of reflection are based on epistemic stances or our beliefs about the nature of knowledge (King and Kitchener, 2004). For example, do we seek knowledge from experts? Or are there types of knowledge where truths are relative to the specific situations where they occur? While some knowledge may be absolute, we know enough about the process of human development to understand that the effects of teaching practices vary according to the different characteristics of the learner, the contextual factors in the school or classroom, and the specific aspects of the content being taught. This is why we know that there is no teaching strategy that works all the time with all students. Teacher agency requires that a teacher have an openness to question everything and to understand that our professional knowledge is relative to the context and to our own way of interpreting our experiences.

Mezirow (1998) explains that such an open stance leads the individual to reflect critically. To him, critical reflection entails the examination of one's own assumptions, such as questioning knowledge, research, findings, assumptions, and perspectives about how the world works. Critically reflective teachers analyze their own meaning perspectives, which are taken for granted assumptions about the world. For teachers, the process then entails examination of professional experiences, while being open to the possibility that what is believed to be true may be wrong. Or through critical reflection, teachers may realize that accepted school practices might be inappropriate for specific situations in the teaching and learning work in the classroom. Perhaps, a specific practice that has been effective so many times before will not work with one or more specific students now.

## Transformation of Meaning Perspectives

This ability to question the validity of beliefs that are considered true is crucial in critical reflection, and it can lead to transformative learning because it allows new understandings to emerge. It leads to development of new levels of professionalism and creates the space where decision making can improve practices. Yet, teachers have been socialized to follow directions and to obey the policies and mandates. Their work is evaluated based on how their students fare on standardized state exams. So how can we transform teachers' reflective thinking to include the critical stance necessary for them to make decisions that are based on logical reasoning and critical reflection? According to Mezirow (1998), this transformation requires the presence of dissonances between assumptions and experiences, or beliefs and reality, which can only occur through careful analysis and evaluation.

Although extensive research in teacher education has focused on the development of reflective thinking, transformative learning theory has not been widely applied. We have developed an understanding of how the transformative process can be facilitated through extensive research built on the work of Mezirow as explained by Steven Hodge (2011). Critical reflective thinking can promote transformation in assumptions especially when facilitated through social practices and working structures that allow for it to take place. It can emerge from communities of practice in school settings and can be the product of practitioner inquiry.

We can surmise that the process of critical reflection of teaching requires a context where teachers feel safe to question their practices and the policies and mandates within the school structure. Cultural-historical theory can inform the work of promoting teacher critical reflection and an inquiry stance that can lead to professional development through agency.

## TEACHER AGENCY THROUGH CULTURAL-HISTORICAL THEORY

The cultural-historical approach is based on a theory of human development as explained by Lev Vygotsky and Alexander Luria, after their extensive research during the early part of the twentieth century. The theory focuses on human development as emerging from social interactions and notes the important contributions that society makes to individual development. In this theory, human consciousness is primarily founded in the social dimension (Vygotsky, 1980), and mental processes in individuals emerge out of participation in social life. In simple terms, as argued by Vygotsky, we become ourselves through others. Our way of thinking is based on processes that were imported into our minds and became a part of our mental functioning (Wertsch, Tulviste, and Hagstrom 1993, pp. 340–41).

Learning, then, is the result of mediation, or specific actions that lead individuals to acquire new understandings that fit within their social contexts. Lave and Wenger (1991), who examined the way novices became established members of informal groups, explain how thinking and new understandings are mediated in three ways:

1. Scaffolding, or actions that assist the learner in moving to new forms of understanding.

2. Cultural interpretations, where knowledgeable others help the novice acquire new understandings by connecting what is already known to new material.
3. Collective interpretations that are generated by a group of experts and novices with different areas of expertise and perspectives. As the group interprets situations to resolve the problems or contradictions between what they learn and actual practice, they jointly develop new knowledge and tools to address challenges.

A way to understand the cultural-historical approach to the development of professional agency in teachers is to examine four components that interconnect to promote development: context, identity, positionality, and activity.

## Development in Context

A basic principle in the cultural-historical approach is that learning, or development, is mediated by what is termed *cultural activities* (Vygotsky, 1978). In other words, development embodies not just the rote memorization of bits of information but also an appropriation through interactions with others, or activities engaged in within a context. To fully comprehend the development of teacher agency, we need to understand the tensions between the context and the individual. As explained by Cole, Engeström, and Vasquez (1997), the context is not predetermined but is made up of the "mutually constituted, constantly shifting, situational definitions that are accomplished through the interactional work of the participants" (p. 6). This means that we need to understand how the individual, as a professional, is positioned within the specific context of the workplace, in this case, the school setting.

An example of how the professional context promotes agency is made evident by Farris-Berg, Dirkswager, and Junge (2012), who completed a case study of eleven schools where teachers have a high level of what they call autonomy. This study examines schools where teachers collectively make decisions that affect the overall success of the school. The decision-making power of the teachers as a collective, based on eight specific practices, includes not only making decisions about learning curriculum and technology but also selecting, evaluating, and terminating their colleagues' employment to meet objectives set by the group.

The inventory of teacher-powered schools (Teacher-Powered Schools, 2017), first presented in this research, has evolved from the eight original practices to fifteen. Information about the teacher-powered approach can be found online at the Teacher-Powered Schools website (https://www.teacherpowered.org/inventory). It is commendable that the awareness of promoting teacher decision making is growing nationwide. Through this study, we see that, when given the power to make decisions, teachers emulate the characteristics of high-performing organizations, such as accepting ownership for results and setting and measuring their progress toward goals. It is also crucial to note here that the teachers, as a collective group of professionals, have the charge of goal setting for the school and the means of assessing the progress toward these goals.

With the findings in this study, we see that professional development activities and the evolution of working practices within a school can indeed be led by the teachers and instructional leaders together. In this kind of setting, their collective work serves as a means of acculturating new teachers into decision making as part of the teaching profession. Of course, there is also an individual interpretation that takes place in each classroom as a result of the individual's professional values and the specific factors within each classroom. However, even the individual interpretation and resulting modes of action are in some ways influenced by the social context of the school.

These concepts for creating a context of collaboration have been expanded and applied to the framework called communities of practice (COP). Wenger (1999) details specific principles that can be applied to such working contexts as schools. Though not specifically developed for the promotion of teacher agency, the principles of COP can be applied. This is further explained in chapter 6, which focuses on how teacher educators and school administrators can promote teacher agency in educational settings. Thus, through the application of cultural-historical theory, the development of a set of professional skills is a function of how it is applied to the structures of the work environment.

## Development of Professional Identity

For teachers, professional development is the appropriation of knowledge and skills that will eventually be applied based not only on the context of the work setting but also on the individual's identity. In other words, learning new skills does not automatically lead to its application; the application depends on the individual's values and perspectives about knowledge and learning and the teacher's professional identity.

In simple terms, teachers' professional identities refers to how teachers define themselves or their sense of themselves as professionals. We develop an identity by associating with particular groups, beliefs, and ways of being and by rejecting other practices. Our individual identity is the nexus where we negotiate our different ways of being in the world. Professional identities have been identified as concepts or images of self that strongly influence the way individuals develop as teachers (Beijaard, Meijer, and Verloop, 2004). It also includes what individual teachers find important in their professional work and lives based on their experiences and society's views of what a teacher is. Identities are forged from the set of values that a person accumulates through a lifetime of experiences.

We can conceptualize professional identities for teachers as emergent first from their own experiences as students, when they were children, and then continuously developing through preservice preparation and finally through in-service development as they engage in their work within their particular school, which has its own working culture and social norms. Because professional actions are founded on the interaction between personal and professional values, teacher professional identity begins first through interactions with caregivers and then in schools through interactions with schoolteachers, as documented by Lortie (2002).

Therefore, professional identity formation is not a simplistic, linear process but is dependent on the life histories and experiences of each teacher, along with the pedagogical knowledge acquired in teacher preparation. Furthermore, the professional development continues as the teacher enters the profession, and this development is affected by the sociocultural factors of the teacher's personal and professional life, as well as ability and choice to exercise agency.

The relationships between agency and identity have been documented in research (Edwards, 2007; Kayi-Aydar, 2015). Through the use of positioning theory (Davies and Harré, 1999), Kayi-Adar defines the construction of identity as a social process that is dynamic and constantly changing as individuals position themselves in relation to others. In addition to self-assigned positionality, agency is the result of how others assign positions to the individual.

For example, in the schools described by Farris-Berg, Dirkswager, and Junge (2012), teachers actively engage in decision making as part of their work because they have been positioned to make collective decisions within the work environment at these specific schools. In their study, they describe how teachers make such decisions as deciding on a curriculum to meet the needs of the students in their particular context. The kind of work carried out by teachers in these schools places them in a position of power not normally possible in other schools because, within the context of most schools, professional identity does not normally include this high level of agency.

In their book, Farris-Berg, Dirkswager, and Junge (2012) describe a teacher who had been chosen to work at one of the schools in the study and who at first felt uncomfortable engaging in the decision-making work that had been established by the teaching workforce. However, through social practices and the routines established at that school, the new teacher eventually transformed her professional practice to include the agentic acts that were a part of the school culture because she eventually chose to assign herself the position of decision maker that had first been assigned to her by her peers. It is important to consider that teacher agency cannot be imposed; the individual must make the choice to exercise agency.

Though they used the term *teacher autonomy*, Farris-Berg, Dirkswager, and Junge (2012) present cutting-edge work on teacher agency. Through their research, they clearly explain what can be accomplished when the school context includes teacher agency as part of the normal way of working. Ideally, we want to see teacher agency as a systemic part of the teaching profession. Nevertheless, teacher agency can also be accomplished to some degree within specific classrooms, if the conditions are right and spaces are created to allow individual teachers to engage in decision making based on positionality. In either case, teachers must have the perspective that decision making is part of their work and thus a part of their professional identity.

## Positionality in the Development of Agency

An important factor to consider is the individual's ability to position himself or herself in relation to others within the working context. Positionality depends on an individual's values and beliefs about their right to make decisions about their actions within a social context. In addition, an individual's culture and sense of self influences their willingness to take on a position of power. Therefore, cultural values play an important role in the formation of professional values and should be considered when we develop teacher-preparation models, especially as we aim to diversify the teacher workforce, currently an area of concern (U.S. Department of Education, 2016).

The educational model at Boricua College, presented in the beginning of this chapter, is an example of teacher preparation that addresses this concern. The college's educational model across all of their programs was primarily created to meet the educational needs of Puerto Ricans in New York City. Its dialogical approach allows for students to engage in self-directed learning (Knowles, 1988) with the support of educational facilitators.

Within this context, students are guided to become aware of their personal values that have been affected by their culture and to engage in the process of constructing their identities by integrating their personal and professional values in unique ways. This educational model allows for individuals to forge their own identities, engaging them during the preservice phase in agentic acts that prepare them for a high level of decision making. This is especially significant because, through this educational program, these students experience socially just pedagogies that value them as individuals and empower them to engage in the construction of their own professional identities. This kind of empowerment is a prerequisite for agency, and it can exist either through self-positioning or through the positioning assigned by more-powerful others. For marginalized populations, it is crucial to create contexts where the individuals can experience the act of positioning themselves so they can exercise agency based on the understanding that it is their right.

The relationship between positioning and the formation of identities is also illustrated in research conducted by Kelly (2006). This study presents the development of professional identity as a process mediated through initial professional training as well as the political and social context of the profession and the structures of the workplace. According to Kelly, teacher identity constantly evolves through a process of negotiation of membership in social communities as experiences are interpreted. In other words, it evolves from engagement and participation with others.

Thus, professional identities exist in the interplay between how we see ourselves in response to the actions of others toward us. Furthermore, it evolves from our social construction of ourselves as we relate to other professionals in our milieu. Therefore, how a teacher acts is a function of their professional identity and the way they position themselves or are positioned by others within the work context or the structures within school systems. Learning is then an incremental process that is socially shared, and skills that are mastered and internalized become part of the individual's way of thinking.

In school structures within the current accountability mandates, we can clearly see that school systems mediate teachers' work based on the available tools and signs within these structures, which limit the engagement in teacher agency. In cultural-historical theory, the words *tools* and *signs* have special meanings. They refer to the artifacts within a social context (*tools*) and the language of the specific culture (*signs*).

In teachers' work, tools include curriculum materials, teacher guides, and the specific instructional materials that facilitate work for specific outcomes. The signs include the specialized vocabulary used by teachers to communicate among themselves about the work of teaching. Within the current context of schools, the most-salient outcome is in the form of high-stakes test scores. The signs and tools in the high-stakes accountability context mediate the actions of teachers and limit their agency.

In sum, if agency is mediated by the interaction between the individual and the tools and structures within the social setting, in this case, the school structures, then an individual's ability to exercise agency for change within this context can only take place by using the cultural tools and resources available. In this theoretical view of teacher agency, the context plays a major role in how agency is shaped because individual actions are always mediated by the tools within the context and by the beliefs and values that are formed in relation to the social context (Wertsch, 1993).

There are studies that make use of cultural-historical theory to examine the development of agency by analyzing its relationships to context and identity formation. For example, Lasky (2005) finds that teachers are active agents, some choosing to act passively and others actively. Their actions, then, are mediated or facilitated not only by structures within the school setting, such as the norms within a school and the externally mandated policies, but also by their perception of themselves as teachers.

Lasky's work is significant because it examines the relationships between agency, identity, and vulnerability, which is a state of being that interacts with beliefs, values, and a sense of self-confidence. The study focuses on the mediation of teacher agency within collective settings and shows that agency can be promoted within an environment of trust, where understandings, values, and goals are shared and where teachers collaborate on new, shared understandings of their professional work.

Conversely, Lasky states that agency is stifled when externally generated reforms, such as the emphasis on performance as measured by high-stakes assessments, are in opposition to the teachers' professional values about what constitutes good education for their students. In this kind of work environment, teachers succeed when they primarily satisfy the definitions of their work that come from administrators or policy makers, and teachers' vulnerability is heightened while agency is diminished. Furthermore, the study suggests that the political, social, and economic systems in education may have deep and enduring effects on the formation of teachers' identities, which may explain why many teachers today prefer to leave decision making to the educational leaders in their schools.

## Activity and Development through the CHAT Perspective

From the studies described thus far, it is clear that development and work depend on related factors. A specific branch of cultural-historical theory that examines the way work structures and individuals interact is called cultural-historical activity theory (CHAT) (Roth and Lee, 2007). It is the foundation of much research to promote change in work practices driven by practitioners.

Haapasaari, Engeström, and Kerosuo (2016) applied the CHAT methodology in a study that is of particular significance to school leaders, though it was not specifically conducted within a school setting, because it focused on transformation from an organizational perspective rather than from the individual perspective. It is important to note that, through the use of the CHAT framework, the unit of analysis in studies of agency always looks at the individual within the surrounding social context, not the individual in isolation (Wertsch, 1993, p. 342). Thus, the CHAT framework helps us to understand how collective activity can promote or hinder teacher agency within school structures.

The study by Haapasaari, Engeström, and Kerosuo (2016) examined the emergence of transformative agency in the workers as a collective. They define transformative agency as one that emerges from examining problems and contradictions within collective settings and the way activities or work practices are carried out. The findings reveal that transformative agency is dependent on employees taking an active role that leads to profound changes in the work of organizations. Further, it was discovered that transformative agency evolves with interactions and leads to a dynamic, long-lasting process of development.

These findings have profound implications for educational transformation. We can deduce from this study that school transformations need to be driven by the teachers, not the educational leaders. Therefore, if we want to improve educational practices, we must allow teachers as a collective group to identify the problems in their specific schools and classrooms and to develop new practices collectively through their own research. The role of the school leaders in this approach would be to guide the process while allowing teachers to develop the objectives and the means of achieving them. The findings in this study further explain why and how the teacher-powered schools described by Farris-Berg, Dirkswager, and Junge (2012) work.

To connect the CHAT framework to school systems in particular, we turn to Anne Edwards (2007). Her extensive research was conducted within the context of a tightly controlled school reform in England and examined ways to promote agentic actions in teachers as they worked within the school system. In particular, she developed the concept of relational agency, defined as the capacity to seek and give support to others, especially within the work setting. She found that relational agency could only be present when the environment does not encourage dependency. Rather, it emerges in formal and informal settings, allowing participants to work with others to achieve a specific objective or to promote transformation within them. In particular, we find that her use of the CHAT framework elucidates how the collective intersects with the individual and allows us to understand how to promote teacher agency in a relational approach.

As explained by Edwards (2007), relational agency requires three elements:

1. mutual responsibility,
2. object-oriented activity, and
3. the wider relevance of relational agency.

Mutual responsibility focuses on meaning making that includes the perspectives of others. While this concept evolved from the work of Goldstein (1999), where teachers and learners work together in the learning and meaning-making processes, we can also argue for the inclusion of teachers with other teachers in the process of meaning making. Object-oriented activity refers to the centrality of the collective objectives. In other words, though agency is valued, it is limited to agentic acts that will lead to the achievement of the collective objectives. This relates to the wider relevance of agency, for it has a directionality that is purposeful for the collective, not just the individual. In other words, within schoolwork, there are educational objectives that the school as a whole is working toward, such as academic success of all students.

The CHAT framework also has implications for teacher education. In this case, the collective activity can take place within the context of a university course or a teacher-preparation program. An example of how agency emerges as part of the teacher professional identity during the preservice phase is illustrated in a study by Lipponen and Kumpulainen (2011), where the teacher educators and preservice teachers engaged in collective inquiry that led to the examination of theoretical knowledge about practices and the development of pedagogically powerful practices that were then applied in the field setting.

## TEACHER AGENCY THROUGH CRITICAL PEDAGOGY

Finally, it is imperative that we consider critical pedagogy and Freire (2013) in particular when developing a theoretical framework for the facilitation of teacher agency as an integral part of the professional identities of teachers. Teachers have been marginalized and are in need of conscientization before they can engage in decision making. The term *conscientization* refers to the process of becoming aware of or critically conscious of the political and social forces that have led to our present reality. In the conscientization process, one reflects and gains new knowledge about the nature of our social conditions by uncovering their real causes and engaging in actions with the intention of transforming the concrete existential situations.

The implication from the research done by Lipponen and Kumpulainen (2011) is that teacher educators ought to engage in pedagogical inquiry with their preservice teachers, which in turn can lead to the development of strong professional identities where professional agency is one component. To achieve this in teacher preparation, the coursework should veer away from traditional models, where activities are controlling and commanding. Rather, they should include an instructional style that connects with students (future teachers) as subjects who engage with dialogical, reciprocal interactions and distributes responsibilities, where the educator and the students interact as members of a learning community. In this fashion, learning is the result of a collective negotiation. Only then can we foster the necessary stance to engage in professional practices from a perspective where the learners are active "subjects confronted with the world . . . engaged in invention and reinvention" (Freire 2013). This exemplifies the value of critical pedagogy.

Joan Wink (2000) makes this abstract concept crystal clear as we seek the best ways to facilitate the professionalization of teachers as critical pedagogues. For her, the conscientization process allows "teachers to have confidence in their own knowledge, abilities, and experiences" (Wink, 2000). She further illustrates critical pedagogy as being transformative through an illustration created by one of her preservice teachers. Critical pedagogy is transformative because, through this kind of learning, teachers can become decision makers and creators of their own practices

## A COMBINED THEORETICAL FRAMEWORK

In our understanding of teacher agency as a crucial characteristic in the professionalization of teachers, it is important to consider adult learning and cultural-historical theories. Additionally, as we seek to understand the development of agency as a part of the teacher professional identity, we must also infuse our practices with principles of critical pedagogy in order to help teachers achieve conscientization and transform our society into a place that promotes the development of freedom and democracy. Through critical pedagogy, we can help teachers become aware of the forces behind the school structures and policies that can prevent them from exercising their agency as they work with students.

*Part II*

# Teacher Agency in Practice

> "Teaching should be your hobby. You have to love what you do, be selfless, and look for new ways to engage students. As a teacher, you also have to be a researcher and never stop learning about what you can do for your students."—Lileana Ríos-Ledezma

This quote was made by a teacher at the end of her first year of teaching in elementary school during one of the semistructured interviews between myself, a university professor, and Lileana, author of the chapter 4 in this book. The interviews became part of a five-year narrative study.

While part I of the book is theoretical in nature, part II presents teacher agency in practice. Chapter 4 presents teacher agency from the perspective of a teacher who was first a participant in narrative research but who eventually became a collaborator and engaged in an analysis of her own narratives. It is important to mention that, because this chapter makes use of a self-study methodology, it is written in the first-person perspective, unlike the other parts of the book.

Lileana describes her practices and agentic acts as a third- and fifth-grade teacher within the context of a public school in south Texas, a setting that is generally embedded with systems that limit teachers' abilities to make decisions. Nevertheless, due to a not commonly held set of professional values that affected this teacher's professional identity, she was able to exercise agency beyond the limits experienced by many teachers today. Her account provides us with a deep understanding of how teacher agency can be exercised with positive results, even amid the current high-accountability system.

Chapter 5 builds on the work presented in chapter 4. It provides practical advice to teachers so they can make decisions within their classrooms and exercise some level of agency in their professional practice, even within the current conditions of public schools, where agency is generally not a part of the work environment.

Chapter 6 closes the book with suggestions for the promotion of teacher agency and transformation of the teaching professional identity. It is specifically written for school leaders and teacher educators and offers suggestions for the creation of spaces for teacher agency within schools. The discussion makes clear connections to the theoretical principles presented in chapter 3.

*Chapter Four*

# Teacher Agency

*One Teacher's Journey*

Lileana Ríos-Ledezma

> "He said, 'What were your grades on the state test that you all took on Thursday?' I said, 'Well, I only had two kids fail. . . . [T]hey both have dyslexia, but I've been working with them. . . . I have a 94%.' . . . And then he gives me an evaluation online, and he's like, 'I would really want to see more whole group instruction . . . showing them eight to ten problems and then go over them and then do another eight to ten problems and then go over it.' And I'm like, 'Hah? All day? My kids will die, you know!'"

Over the years, the teaching profession has changed drastically due to the pressure of testing accountability. Many educators find themselves in a quandary as they struggle to comply with the demands to increase test scores, as seen in my narrative at the start of this chapter, and their personal values or desires to effectively teach students to learn. In fact, some school districts have even been known to initiate compensatory programs to entice teachers and staff into obtaining high marks on state assessments at all costs. Subsequently, the stressful nature of reaching passing standards for schools has essentially stripped the idea of teacher agency from the classroom and enforced an intervention, "drill and kill" mentality.

Teachers oftentimes are cornered with directives about the type of instruction they are required to implement due to the focus on testing accountability. Sadly enough, one cannot fathom how the act of teaching no longer lies in the hands and heart of the expert: the teacher. It is undeniably important to provide preservice and in-service teachers with essential knowledge in order to begin to establish teacher agency in their classrooms and schools. The freedom to exercise control or make decisions within the context of school district mandates has become a daunting task, forcing many educators to comply with policies or seek other career paths.

On my newly found journey down the educational path, I asked myself, What could be done to exercise this freedom to teach? Were there ways in which teachers could truly gain autonomy? Would I be consumed by the test-taking craze and forgo my teaching philosophy of sound pedagogy? Or, would I be able to stand strong and hold onto the core principles that had led me to choose teaching as my profession?

Surely, in the era of high-stakes testing, a first-year teacher would succumb to the overwhelming pressure to "teach to the test" and obediently remain silent as teacher agency is essentially stripped from the classroom. As a novice teacher, I was determined to bring passion, love, and curiosity back to the teaching field at the height of such accountability craze. In my self-reflective journey of professional growth, I was fortunate to discover how to establish a culture for learning; to implement engaging activities within high-stakes-testing grade levels; and, most of all, how to achieve teacher agency.

Looking at my past years of teaching and using a self-study methodology, I was able to uniquely examine reoccurring themes within my experiences that explored this phenomenon as both the investigator and participant. This valuable approach allowed me to study my own practices and identify essential characteristics for developing teacher agency in a restrictive period in education (LaBoskey, 2009). Additionally, only by critically analyzing my own practices through reflective dialogues, I was able to identify characteristics needed to begin a path to teacher agency.

This self-study evolved throughout five years, during which I engaged in various interactions with key constituents: my students, parents, administrators, and mentor. The interactions I had allowed me to expand my thinking and systematically reflect on the actions I took on my journey to achieving teacher agency. To be clear, I must state that the development of this self-study used multiple self-reflections and explorations of my practices in order to provide teachers with genuine experiences that could lead them to reach autonomy in their own classrooms.

In this chapter are snapshots of the copious discussions with my mentor, professor, and friend and reflective thoughts that occurred during my first five years of teaching. Through her guidance and our meetings, which took place twice a year for the first five years of my professional career, I had the opportunity to discuss daily struggles, student achievements, and questions I still had regarding teaching practices. These meetings were established at the beginnings and ends of every school year.

In all sincerity, I viewed our gatherings as a privileged mentorship, an opportunity to reflect about my actions as a teacher; as time passed, it was clear that a partnership had developed between us. My mentor strategically delved deeper, asking leading questions and making comments about the amount of freedom I had developed within my first year of teaching, as evidenced in a statement she made on one occasion: "[Y]ou're supposed to have academic freedom, which means you follow the state standards, but how you teach is completely up to you."

I was able to provide an insight from the trenches, and soon we realized it had become necessary to share this self-study with educators. Those who struggle to obtain their freedom to teach could explore the qualities and conditions I used to obtain teacher agency within the field of education. With so many teachers looking for the ability to teach according to their own expertise, our research has become significant to all who work with students of all ages.

## METHOD AND FINDINGS

In order to provide transparency, validation, and trustworthiness for the words on this page, all raw transcriptions of our meetings were taped, transcribed, and analyzed. Our data collection consisted of 189 pages of transcribed audio recordings of ten narrative sessions that focused on my reflections of the past year (accomplishments, challenges and successes, lessons learned) and objectives for the next academic year. Interestingly enough, the findings shed light on how teacher agency could be reached by an educator with little to no experience in the teaching field. Upon reviewing the transcriptions numerous times during the process of coding and recoding (Anfara, Brown, and Mangione, 2002), an emergent theme in the dialogue was my capacity to exercise agency. This led to a closer examination in the final analysis at the conclusion of the data collection.

Further analysis confirmed the elements crucial to my development of teacher agency. Such elements were identified and coded appropriately when situations in my career similarly supported my search for teacher agency or my freedom to teach. Once certain characteristics were identified, I shared them with my collaborating researcher (the author of this book), who examined my findings, asked clarifying questions, and guided me in the analytical process. Credibility and dependability of my research were achieved through a process of using the code-recode strategy, where I identified key characteristics throughout the transcripts collected over five years (Anfara, Brown, and Mangione, 2002).

A code-mapping analysis similarly used by Anfara, Brown, and Mangione (2002) was employed to establish validity within this self-study. The first iteration, or thorough read of the transcripts, shed light on multiple situations in which I felt I had demonstrated a degree of teacher agency. Subsequent reads indicated an existence of patterns between the situations. These patterns formed connections between instances first identified and provided an overarching motif. After the third iteration, an in-depth analysis and review of the transcripts yielded essential characteristics I had exhibited during my first five years of teaching.

## Passion

As important as the content knowledge needed to teach is the passion required to spark interest and the joy of learning. Merriam-Webster's dictionary (2017) defines *passion* as a "strong feeling of enthusiasm or excitement for something or about doing something." Additionally, I define *passion* as what drives a teacher to work with twenty-plus students and teach more than the required curriculum, more hours than stated in the contract, and make less money than others with similar amount of preparation (Tucker, 2017). A good friend once blatantly stated, "If I don't become a marine biologist, I'll just be a teacher." I was dumbfounded. How had my career, *my teaching career*, become someone's fallback? Surely, as in other professions, teaching required expertise, talent, and passion.

Throughout my first five years as a teacher, I found passion to be an essential element on my journey to attain teacher agency within my school and school district. Passion was an intrinsic desire to go above and beyond the normal standards required of a person, in this case, a teacher. An important element of passion is how I connected personally with my students. I shared with them things I did that I thought could be interesting (or perhaps inspiring) and connected it to math and the different centers, called workshop, as exemplified in the following quote from a transcript:

> I had told them that I was going to New York, . . . and . . . yeah, they were really excited about it. Well, I went over there to take pictures of the museum, . . . the Empire State Building, you know, the Statue of Liberty, and I came back and showed them a PowerPoint of it. . . . Well, they got to connect, and they were like, "*Wow*, look! That's the Empire State Building." And I'm like, "Yeah, this is where the World Trade Center was," and I showed them Ground Zero and [said], "One of these days, you all could go over there, but you have to stay focused in school because it's a little expensive," and I was showing them the subway and stuff like that. And then I said, "Guess what? We're gonna have a New York–style workshop." [They said,] "Yaaay!" and there were math problems, but they were about New York. For example, You know, the Empire State Building is 1,872 feet tall, the Rockefeller Center is this, this . . . tall. How much taller or how many more feet [does this building have]?

This is an example of how passion was fruitful in teaching. This passion allowed me to go above and beyond, to advocate for my students and exercise teacher agency in the selection of my teaching practices and methods. My students were engaged in their learning because I was *invested* in my teaching. In my passion, students knew I cared about them, and they began to care about their own learning.

Passion also led me to always think outside the box, sometimes spending extra money to create the conditions that would lead to the desired outcomes; engaged students; and, ultimately, success in learning. One way was to create the environment and activities that were kid friendly and relevant. The following excerpt from a transcript illustrates this point:

> Well, it's funny. I moved three times since I've been there. . . . Every classroom that I moved in I painted. Well this last one is dear to me because I painted so beautifully. . . . It's on Facebook. It's green and purple, lime green and . . . purple.
>
> **Dr. O:** The first one was aqua?
>
> [Yes]. My second was green and blue, like a lime green with the dark blue. . . . I was doing science that year, so I thought green/blue, ocean, land, water. [This year] I said, "[Y]ou know what? I need it to be . . . eye popping," . . . and it looks really, really nice.

My sincere passion for teaching urged me to create a pleasant, kid-friendly space for learning, even if I had to do it myself and spend my own money. Throughout much of my transcripts, I stated that "I often spent countless hours . . . looking for different things . . . always spending extra [time and money] . . . at the Dollar Store trying [to find items to enhance my teaching] . . . because you have to get [students'] attention." Why did I spend countless hours furnishing my classroom, purchase additional materials for lessons, and work endlessly at school and from my home? There was a passion, a strong feeling of excitement inside of me to ignite motivation for learning and, above all, make learning fun!

Later, reflecting on my own passion, I came to realize that it was effective in that it was contagious. My passion inspired my students to have a passion for learning. This was evident when they often eagerly walked into the classroom, placed their backpacks on their assigned hooks, and read the objective written on the board, which provided a preview of the lesson for the day. My students expected to learn and have fun while doing so.

When we learned about mathematical arrays, my students were excited to create "arrays with stickers . . . [creating] rows by columns with stickers . . . and computing the product." In contrast to my progressive methods, I observed many teachers follow the district-suggested lesson plans, use the state-adopted textbooks, and print off worksheet after worksheet. I constantly asked myself, Couldn't teaching be more fun? My students and I certainly thought so! Some teachers were born to teach, while others found teaching along the way as a means for a steady paycheck, and so they followed the rules set forth and gave no more or no less.

The passion my students demonstrated during their time spent learning in my classroom became obvious schoolwide. Students were engaged in learning, eager to return to the classroom after recess, and motivated to read! By the middle of the year, my team teacher, or partner, commented on the amazing behavior our students were showing. One morning, after announcements had been made and our math lesson was about to begin, my team teacher called me out of my classroom so that I could witness every reading teacher's dream come true: "All the students were sitting comfortable around the room, chapter book in hand, and completely engaged in reading." How did we know they were engaged? Not one pair of eyes had looked up from their novels. In my transcript, I vividly described the scene:

> I had to take a picture of them because after "books for breakfast" . . . after breakfast they're supposed to read. . . . The kids . . . already know [what to do]. Well, I go [to] Mr. Mathew's class and tell him the agenda for the day [different things we had planned], . . . and then [he said,] 'I think something is going on.' . . . I'm like, 'What do you mean?' He said, 'Come and see,' and we peeked in the classroom, and all the students had a chapter book. . . . They were all [focused on] reading, and it (was) quiet. . . . Some of them had their legs on top of the table. . . . And [Mr. Mathew] goes, 'I just gave Luis a paper to take to the office, and I handed it to him, and this is what he did.' [He showed me how.] He was reading the paper, he didn't even look at it [the form], and he put the book down, like [not] wanting to have his eyes off the book, and he walked out, came back, and just went back to his book.

It was amazing! Gazing in awe at the beautiful image of our students, my team teacher mentioned to me that he could not recall seeing such motivated readers in his twenty years of teaching. I knew I had sparked a passion for learning in my students and reignited a passion for teaching in him. Toward the end of that year, he thanked me for reminding him how fun teaching was supposed to be! In my narrative, I retold the story of how my mentor teacher approached me and said,

> He was thankful I had come into his life. I had reminded him why he had become a teacher and revived his passion for teaching. As a part of an end-of-the-year activity, we—my students, team teacher, and I—wrote short letters to each other. He wrote a letter in which he stated that I helped him [reignite] his passion. . . . He had just completed his fifteen years of teaching.

Fortunately, we were able to work together a few years after that, and it was always the same passion for our students that drove us to have a successful year! Because of our passion, we were able to execute our own teaching methods and coordinate special events, such as read-a-thons, multiplication bees, and marble machine competitions! Other teachers, later convinced that the passion driving my classroom could be replicated by a simple implementation of my ideas of "workshop," asked me for details on the type of workshop activities I had established in my classroom.

I first learned about workshop through my sister, who had also been a teacher. It could best be explained as "individualized centers" in which the students could take the supplies needed from a specified area and work to complete their work anywhere they'd wish around the room. These workshops typically contained engaging items that required them to use colored paper, stamps, fraction pieces, and so on. The kids were raving about my workshop activities, and teachers thought that, if I gave them details about what it entailed, students would be keener on completing the work in their classroom, as well. Of course, I was absolutely overjoyed to share my ideas about workshop and how it should be established in the classroom, but I knew that, without overwhelming passion and love for teaching, their students would see right through the act.

At the end of my first year as a teacher, my principal also asked me to share my structure on workshop with the entire grade level and assigned me the title of grade-level chair, which meant I was going to lead teachers of my grade level and guide the decision making for the grade. While I did get many unconvinced looks about being a new teacher on campus and sharing my ideas for a well-structured, highly engaged classroom, I felt confident that my first year had been a success, and my students' passion for learning was living proof! The fact that I was a new teacher did not mean I did not know any better. I learned that, when students are motivated to come to your class to learn, *that* is success, and I had accomplished that! I was and continue to be passionate about the students and the learning that occurred under my watch.

## Giving

At times, teaching can be a very expensive hobby and requires a giving spirit. Teachers often feel they actually get paid less than minimum wage because they are always spending their own money on items to improve their instruction. Like most teachers, a good portion of my paycheck went toward buying more supplies, books, or games for the classroom. A giving spirit often drove me to spend my personal money to supply the paint to bring color into my classroom. My spending even occurred in other states while on vacation!

The trinkets I purchased were always used to engage students and most of all establish real-life meaningful connections. I will never forget the math lesson called "Math: New York Style" after I had taken a spring break trip to New York with my family. The time I spent having an authentic discussion with my students was essential; most of them had never left the Rio Grande

Valley in Texas and were thrilled to see pictures of such a place as New York City. Students were excited to learn about the different sights in New York, and all were overjoyed to complete math lessons I had created involving the Statue of Liberty, Madison Square Garden, and the Empire State Building. These workshops were filled with mathematics problems about estimating heights, finding the area, and making change at the local pizzeria.

To close our mathematics workshop lessons for that week, I wanted to end with a memorable experience. I handed out a New York postcard for each and every one of my students, as I explained in the narrative:

> It was so hilarious because I . . . bought everybody a postcard, . . . and I wrote everybody their own little message on the back. . . . I put, "To one of my best students," but everybody had "one of my best," so everyone is my best, and I gave it to them. . . . It had a little personal note, like on Celeste's, I put, "One of these days, you'll own an office here, you know in New York," and she's like, "Oh my God!" I loved it. I loved it so much, and the kids, they really . . . liked doing the workshop, and . . . it made me feel so good. . . . I was so excited to know that they didn't throw them away, you know, that they kept them!

They were thrilled to have a little piece of New York in their hands! For some of them, it was an affirmation of the success they were sure to have on future endeavors if they continued to put forth the effort. For others, it was a word of encouragement to inspire an increase in hard work and dedication. In my transcript, I commented on what this helped me achieve: "[Kids are smart,] and they can see when you give to them generously, . . . not just like food or [snacks], but when [a teacher] give[s] them attention, . . . power [in your classroom]. . . . They respond to you also and they give you power. . . . They give you attention." This giving quality I expressed while teaching helped me gain trust and love from my students, who were then willing to give me their attention, respect, and, ultimately, trust.

It is important that I emphasize that a giving spirit did not always indicate a need for a monetary expense; it often meant that I gave of my understanding, time, and effort. One year, I had an extremely challenging group. I had started the year as the State of Texas Assessments of Academic Readiness (STAAR) teacher. STAAR is our high-stakes accountability measures. The STAAR teacher was a different position that required me to help other teachers resolve classroom issues and mentor the delivery of their lessons so their students would pass the tests. However, when the school suddenly experienced a surge in the number of fifth-grade students, I volunteered to help teach a classroom. I was elated at the idea of having my own classroom again and teaching my own group of students. I felt the surge of excitement knowing I was about to embark on another successful year!

I did not realize it was going to be the most difficult year of my teaching career. Of the twenty-five students in my class, most had experienced difficulties in their home due to parental battles, broken homes, or absent parents. Additionally, some were battling a learning disability and significantly lacked the motivation to focus on schoolwork. My heightened stress level was visible in my narratives that year, as seen here, when I described my process of calling students when they were absent:

> I have a lot of kids in my class, [and often] they're not there, so I call. I call every day after *9 o'clock*, I'm calling a parent, you know, "Good morning, this is Ms. Ríos. I just wanted to know if Victoria is coming in?" "Oh yes ma'am, she will be there right now." And you could tell that they were not gonna be there or that they were asleep or something. I have tardies every day.
>
> I have a little girl. . . . Have you heard in the news [about] the lady that got twenty years? Her husband or her boyfriend beat her two-year-old son and killed him. . . .
>
> And I have the little girl in my class [the sister]. I look at her, and I want to cry because how can I expect her to be worried about prime numbers when her mother . . . is in jail? To me . . . that's not fair for her, you know. . . . There's a lot of kids that need help in that class but not just help academic-wise, but love.

Of course, I did not realize it then, but reflecting on the transcripts now, I was so blessed to have had the privilege to know that particular group of students. Due to the fact that these students were challenging in many ways, it was necessary to take more of my time developing engaging activities to keep their interest. I worked hard to understand their interests and how to work them into the lessons. I dedicated long hours after school and on weekends (as is customary in the teaching field) in order to prepare lessons and set workshops that would entice them. Most importantly, I set time and effort to get to know my students, their personal needs. I gained the support of the school administration, staff, and parents. The trust that developed between the students, school leaders, and parents provided the key I needed to unlock my freedom to teach during that difficult and challenging year. The trust would not have been possible without the giving spirit I demonstrated.

## Breaking the Rules

Of course, the teaching profession has many restrictions, procedures to follow, and mandates from the school district as well as the federal government. In our discussions, my mentor often asked me how I was able to get away with implementing my own lessons, and I responded with, "I ask for forgiveness, not permission." Many times, when teachers realize their students do not understand a concept, drastic measures must be taken, which may involve questionable teaching practices; nothing illegal, of course. Still, such activities would possibly be considered outrageous or superfluous. One morning, I implemented a lesson that was on the cusp of rule breaking:

> So, we [learned about] volume and, we [created] cookies [with] peanut butter and marshmallows, and well, that day my room smelled like peanut butter, . . . like the entire hallway smelled like peanut butter, but the kids were learning about volume, and they understood, you know, volume? . . . And the superintendent walks in my classroom [with my principal], and one thing was [that] we're not supposed to be eating, right? And the second thing, we're not supposed to be doing stuff like that. We're supposed to be doing more worksheets [because testing days were coming]. And it smelled like peanut butter, and he's like, "Hum mm," . . . and then I [said,] "Oooooh," and [one kid said,] "Look at my volume cookie!" . . . I know, and I'm like, "*Oh yeah*," and he's [said,] "Oh, it's so great!" . . . Then the principal walks in right behind him, and she's looking at me, and [I said], "Oh, they're working with volume."
>
> And I mean, . . . I was worried, especially later [when I found out that we were a peanut-free district,] . . . but when she walked in, the kids were able to explain to her what volume was, and the superintendent was able to see that they knew. They understood what they were doing. So, she didn't tell me anything, and as a matter of fact, she told me, "Wow, this is so neat. I've never seen it done like that before."

Of course, the superintendent was speechless. Walking into a classroom of twenty-two accomplished third-graders, it is no wonder he had proceeded to investigate the purpose of our volume cookie lesson. It was obvious by the looks on their faces that some rules had been broken, but neither the principal nor the superintendent could negate that my students were challenged and engaged. No need for worksheets, no need to complete twenty problems from the textbook, no need to beg the students to finish their assignment. All students willingly and energetically completed the task, enjoyed their cookies, and taught the superintendent and our principal how to solve for volume of a regular three-dimensional shape using their volume cookies.

I continued to use that lesson to teach volume for many years after that; however, I did not use peanut butter with my students, as I became aware of the dangerous allergies some students had. My students never forgot the volume cookies; thus, they never forgot what volume meant. Unlike rote learning, authentic and meaningful experiences sparked their interest and transformed learning in my classroom. Furthermore, my principal never reprimanded me for breaking the school rules, seeing that it was evident my students had mastered the objective. I had gained trust, confidence, and teacher autonomy.

Throughout all my years as a teacher, I was able to practice the freedom to teach, even if it meant that I would get a little dirty by practicing some janitorial work. For example, on another occasion, my students had all been introduced to the concept of perimeter, but they were still having trouble showing mastery. After informally assessing, I realized I needed to make learning about perimeter more memorable. After some thinking, it came to me. What could be more memorable than paint?

Washable paint, of course, but paint nonetheless. I looked at the tiled floors in my classroom and only saw an opportunity for students to experience perimeter through art and fun. We would create pieces of art using the tiles on the floor and washable paint. Of course, I began by modeling my own piece of artwork on the floor. I carefully followed the lines of the tiles and painted them a bright green. I created an irregular figure and showed my students how to count the edges to calculate the perimeter.

Students were thrilled to begin constructing their artwork on the floor. A variety of shapes of all colors and sizes began to form, as a large mosaic sprinkled across the classroom floor. Students worked diligently, and as they finished, they were tasked with the challenge of finding the perimeters of their classmates' designs. I didn't give them a requirement. They didn't need one. Students walked freely around the room and talked about the perimeter of their artwork. Everyone was delighted! I could not say the same for the janitors.

The head janitor was horrified when she walked into my classroom later that afternoon. She was speechless and furious. Although I tried to tell her the purpose of having paint all over the floor, she would not hear of it. After apologizing for the added mess, I dared to ask her not to mop for a couple of days to allow the students to revisit the perimeter paintings. I even offered to mop myself in order to make amends.

I had a little visit with our school principal afterward (just to keep her in the loop about the slight confrontation I had had with the keeper of keys)! Fortunately, the principal was very understanding. Because I could explain the purpose of using the floor tiles and paint to help my students understand a concept they had been having trouble with, she promptly assured me that everything would be all right with the head janitor. Of course, everyone in the school heard about my little rendezvous with the head janitor, causing many colleagues to come by to see the children's art on the floor. My students were thrilled with all the publicity, and I was thrilled with their mastery of the concept of perimeter.

## Questioning

In South Texas, there are hardly any seasons: It is either summer or summer, but in education, during the month of March, there is a different season in the air: testing season. Teachers were reteaching the Texas Essential Knowledge and Skills (TEKS), or the state standards, and they were holding boot camps or were preoccupied with "drilling and killing" for the final days before testing. Of course, review was taking place in my classroom; still, the type of learning had not changed. Students were busy bees, writing in their math journals, playing math games, and completing workshops.

My workshops were completely spiraled according to the highest needs of my students. During this time, students worked independently or with a partner of their choice. They often sat comfortably in a corner of the room, on the floor, or on the carpet in the classroom library. They talked, laughed, and, most importantly, learned and reviewed the concepts in a relaxed environment. This happened throughout my years of teaching, but questioning the system was especially challenging in my first year. While I gathered some students for guided math and further differentiation at my teacher table, students around the room were self-guided and self-motivated.

Nonetheless, we were in the midst of testing season, and after a walk-through from my facilitator, I was shocked to hear her feedback regarding my lesson:

> My facilitator said, "You need to do more state assessment prep," and I said, "I'm doing enough prep. You know, this is all [STAAR]." And she's like, "OK, but *more* STAAR [paper and pencil, drill and kill]." and I'm like, "OK," and I just heard what she said, and I kept doing what I was doing. I didn't understand why I couldn't continue doing my workshops. . . . They were addressing the TEKS.

I asked why so many times! Why were they making decisions about my students' needs? Why did they want to see basic worksheet reviews? Subsequently, after more explanations about the importance of reviewing testing questions and how to answer them, I reflected on the workshops my students had been completing. All of my students were working with their partners, exchanging vocabulary terms, and, most of all, learning! I did not want to change workshops to reflect monotonous test preparation. Still, I knew I had to find a compromise in order to continue implementing my own teaching methods.

Before I changed anything about the workshop routine in my classroom, I was fortunate to have the opportunity to speak with my mentor and ask for some advice. She was a university professor, and I knew she would be able to help. I knew that my workshop activities were definitely engaging, purposeful, and focused as a review for the state exam. I had come this far in the school year with the freedom to teach, and I was not keen on giving up on what I thought learning should be.

Thankfully, the advice my professor and mentor offered was brilliant! She suggested that, in order to satisfy *their* hunger for test preparation and review while preserving my fun, hands-on, workshop classroom environment, I could simply add on a paper-pencil accountability task after each workshop. This was the accountability piece that my evaluators were looking for. It was the perfect way to appease the district employees and school administrators whose faith in my nontraditional teaching habits was faltering.

Weeks after that haunting conversation, the day of the test was upon us and, soon after that, the results. My students had done so well that my principal asked me to share my ideas about the structure of workshop to the entire school so that other teachers could replicate it in their classrooms. It was an uphill battle, but the results spoke loud and clear for themselves. Most importantly, from my first year on, I was able to implement my own teaching practices without being questioned about the methods I used in my class! My reputation preceded me, as I was later asked to teach other grade levels. I had stood my ground and pleaded my case, and my students were successful.

## Supportive Administration

> "Every time I went to the principal's office, I was always [given the] OK, . . . so I think if you have the skill to back up what you're gonna do [in your classroom] and see to it that it has a purpose, . . . you'll be fine."

Reflecting on my journey to obtaining teacher agency through statements I made in my narrative, such as this statement, I realized I could not have accomplished the freedom to teach without a supportive administration: a caring principal, a helpful facilitator, and an overall encouraging school district environment. During my five years working at that school, my principal allowed me the freedom to implement my own untraditional practices.

I had a particular way of creating workshop activities that allowed my third- and fifth-graders to learn by manipulating clay into three-dimensional objects, solve multiplication story problems with marshmallow Peeps, and create array word problems and models with stickers! Truth be told, my principal was like all other principals, in that she was concerned with accountability, so every six weeks my students were subjected to a state-released test as practice. My students were doing so well on their practice exams that, during the final weeks before the state test, my principal hardly visited my classroom for observations. The trust had been cemented.

A school's administrative team can either make or break a teacher. I was blessed to have worked in a school district that trusted teachers to do their job. One of my colleagues in another school was not so fortunate. The lack of freedom to teach ultimately drove her to resign from the job midyear through her first year of teaching. I related in this piece of the narrative how, after helping my friend set up some workshops in her classroom, she encountered severe resistance from her school administrators:

> She's [still] upset, and this was a while back, and this was in December. . . . We had set up workshops, all ready, like different math ones, different reading

ones, and when she went back [on Monday], she told the kids, "We're gonna do a workshop today." And she's really cool, you know. And she came in with that idea like, "Oh, . . . we're gonna do a workshop." They [the students] already started thinking like, "This is gonna be fun!" Well, the principal came in, she told [me,] and she got negative feedback, which is what happened to me, too. I got negative feedback, and she called me, she was all disappointed. I said, "No, you just keep doing it." Well the principal came in and [said,] "You need to do interventions during that time." [My friend was not allowed to continue with workshop routines. The freedom to teach] depends on the environment . . . because people have to be flexible. . . . She resigned. They said that the principal [in that school] makes some of . . . the teachers cry every day.

The oppressive environment and lack of academic freedom and teacher choice made the workplace unbearable, thus forcing many teachers to find other school districts and administrative teams that would support their desire to embed creativity, fun, and choice into the school curriculum. Instead, many leave teaching altogether.

## CONCLUSION

In reflecting on my journey to teacher agency, it was evident to me that my passion for teaching and learning provided the platform for me to give all I could to my students without fear of retribution. I dared to question and break the rules to help my students thrive during this age of heightened accountability. Thanks to my principal, I was able to go above and beyond the expectations of a novice teacher to become a strong, independent educator filled with power and the freedom to teach!

*Chapter Five*

# How Can Teachers Exercise Agency?

"The thing I love about education—after the politicians have finished micromanaging; after the think-tank scholars have massaged the latest studies; after the scientists in the Education Department have produced data to justify almost anything—good teachers can still go into their rooms, close their doors and teach."—Winerip, 2011

This statement is often true, as is evident in the self-study presented by Lileana in the previous chapter. Yet school structures often prevent teachers from leading their students into learning. Under the current educational context, teachers are like puppets in a show. They are told how to teach in very specific ways and are manipulated to follow directions without really thinking about them. Then they are held accountable for the results, even though they only followed orders.

The premise is that, if teachers do exactly what they are told, students will achieve high scores on the state assessments. Even though there are differences in the students that may affect the way they perform these tasks, this is rarely considered. Therefore, the assessments given to students are based on erroneous assumptions that hold the teachers accountable for the academic success of students.

Under these conditions, differentiation of instruction is often not implemented successfully, even when it is part of the considerations in instruction, because the curriculum limits the teachers' actions in terms of the content taught, the instructional methods, and the scheduling of activities. When students are not successful, not only are teachers held accountable, but so are the school administrators. In consequence, these educational leaders tend to lay the blame on the teachers. Yet, teachers who are the professionals often could be able to lead students to success if they were allowed to do their craft. The problem lies in that teachers are not given the right to engage in the solution to these problems.

Though school leaders alone create corrective actions to remediate the problems without including the expertise of the teachers in this process, there are some teachers who find ways to do their work and to make the necessary decisions so that their students learn, as described by Michael Winerip in the quote at the start of this chapter. Despite all limitations, *"good teachers can still go into their rooms, close their doors and teach."*

How can teachers engage in decisions about ways to promote learning and a higher level of professionalism? And how can educational leaders create spaces for teacher agency so teachers can be truly held accountable for their actions? Only when teachers are free to play their rightful role as educators of children can they truly be held accountable.

Given the sociocultural and adult learning principles presented in part I of this book, it is obvious that allowing teachers to exercise agency successfully requires a transformation in their professional identities and in the educational context of schools. Considering that accountability measures implemented since the No Child Left Behind Act in 2001 have not led to significant increases in reading, mathematics, or science learning, as demonstrated by national assessments (National Center for Education Statistics, 2013), we obviously need to find a different approach to the education of our nation's future citizens. Furthermore, we have not succeeded in eradicating the achievement gaps between whites and other racial and ethnic groups, nor have we succeeded in eliminating the achievement gap between the rich and the poor.

Hence, it behooves us to significantly change the way we have been engaging in educational policies that have an impact on classroom practices. Within this context, it makes a great deal of sense to engage in dialogue with teachers to seek possible solutions to the educational problems of our nation. This book advocates for the teacher's right to engage in decision making within their classrooms and as part of their work as members of the community of teaching professionals.

There are specific ways to remedy the lack of teacher agency that require the concerted efforts from all types of educators, including teacher educators and school leaders. However, as the call is made to include teachers at the center of all school reform, this chapter precisely addresses teachers in this endeavor and presents suggestions that can lead them to take on an active role in this process. We cannot wait for the desirable systemic changes, for teachers must begin to act toward the needed transformation. This message becomes clearer in the personal perspective in textbox 5.1.

## TEXTBOX 5.1.
## A PERSONAL VIEW

I met a past student the other day while taking my evening walk. She had been my student seven years ago, and I remember her as being creative and passionate when I visited her in her first class. She is indeed a very special teacher and is appreciated by her principal, who allows her to teach in her own style, knowing her students will benefit from her work. After we embraced, happy for the encounter, I asked her how she was and what she was up to. She replied in an almost apologetic tone, "I'm still teaching." For a brief moment, she appeared ashamed of the fact she was still teaching. Then she proceeded to share her latest teaching approaches, clearly enthusiastic about what she had been doing in her classroom.

Why is the idea of remaining in the classroom a reason to feel deflated? It is as if the promotion to other positions in education is the only sign of professional success for teachers. Certainly, medical doctors do not feel unsuccessful if they continue working with patients in their offices for twenty or more years. So, in some ways, teaching still seems to be considered a transitional job, not an aspiring profession. This is truly sad, and I wish to tell all teachers about the incredible value of the teaching profession. All other careers depend on the quality of teachers.

Therefore, teachers, you need to transform the way you see yourselves. First, by embracing your profession with joy and pride, by fully engaging in it with your whole being. This includes connecting with your students and discovering their many talents and challenges. Then, by engaging in self-chosen, continuous professional development, critical thinking, and inquiry. This will allow you to make decisions about the ways to help your students achieve their highest potential. Finally, by sharing your understandings, derived from your inquiry and practices, in ways that will convince others that you are knowledgeable and capable of leading your students. And most of all, you must advocate for what is best for your students based on your knowledge and expertise. All of these acts are part of the profession we call teaching.

## THE ROLE OF THE TEACHER IN TEACHER AGENCY

Though often a myth, it is believed that some choose to teach because they want the summer vacations to rest or because they believe teaching requires less working hours than other professions. Similarly, some people choose to become medical doctors because they like the prestige associated with the title or the possibility of higher pay. It is saddening to hear these kinds of statements, for they diminish the importance of these professions. Like medical doctors, teaching should be a calling; it demands the full engagement of the individual whose acts affect the lives of others.

Fully engaged teachers care for the students in their class, and their profession embodies their whole being, as they maintain their roles beyond working hours. They often think about the best ways to help their students learn and develop into accomplished human beings. They think about tomorrow's class activities and maybe even dream about them. As professionals, they deserve agency. They have the right to teach their students by being given the space to make the most appropriate decisions they know are best for their students. This is because they are at the front line, in full contact with each student as they blossom and struggle to learn and evolve.

The reflection in textbox 5.1 points to the important message in this chapter: Teachers must play a central role in transforming the teaching profession into one that is respected and acknowledged. The previous chapters outline the important elements of teacher agency: why it is crucial, how the historical trajectory of the teaching profession led to its current state, and which theoretical frameworks can be used to promote it. However, the most important person who can transform teaching is the teacher.

Yes, the preparation of teachers to become liberated to engage in professional decision making is of the utmost importance. Also crucial are the spaces created by school leaders where teachers can fully exercise their professional right and their expertise as they lead their students to learning and development to their full potential. These matters are presented in the next and final chapter of this book. However, preparation, professional space, and advocacy for the profession are meaningless if the teachers are not willing to appropriate their role as capable professionals.

Chapter 4 presents a clear example of how teacher agency can be a possibility, as it was exercised by a teacher who successfully made decisions in her classroom. This chapter focuses on specific ways for teachers to engage in agentic acts in the classroom within the current conditions of the educational systems. Of course, it would be wonderful if the school structures were transformed to include teacher agency. This transformation would create a system where teachers can truly engage in inquiry to resolve their teaching challenges or make decisions about how to teach the content assigned to them through standards. Nevertheless, teacher agency can be embraced if it is considered a right and an integral part of the teaching profession or an integral of the professional identity of teachers.

## Forging a Professional Identity

As explained in chapter 3, a teacher's professional identity refers to how teachers define themselves as professionals. Thus, professional identities have been identified as concepts or images of self that strongly influence the way individuals develop as teachers. The professional identity is made up of knowledge, values, and beliefs about the teaching profession and affects everything a teacher does. For example, teacher professional identities lead teachers to

- engage in the careful planning of instruction appropriate for the developmental stages of all the students;
- use their knowledge, skills, and desire to create appropriate learning environments that promote learning and development; and
- engage in inquiry or decision making about ways to address instructional problems.

The last item in this list is often not considered a part of the teachers' identity, though it should be. In essence, though teachers learn a great deal of theory and ways of doing the teaching work, ultimately it is their values and beliefs about what teachers do that really affects the way a teacher works. The identity includes what individual teachers find important in their professional work and lives based on their experiences and society's views of what a teacher is that they accept for themselves (Beijaard, Meijer, and Verloop, 2004; Enedy, Goldberg, and Welsh, 2005).

Professional identities are shaped and reshaped across time (Flores and Day, 2006). Their formation is not a simplistic, linear, or a similar process for all but is dependent on the life histories and experiences of each teacher. It is constructed through experiences that span across time since the beginning of their education and through their professional careers.

A study by Kelly (2006) explains teacher identity as constantly evolving through a process of negotiation of membership in social communities as experiences are interpreted. In other words, it evolves from engagement and participation with others. Thus, professional identities exist in the interplay between how we see ourselves in response to the actions of others toward us, and it evolves from our social construction of ourselves as we relate to other professionals in our milieu. These understandings about the formation of identity can point to the personal choices in the creation of one's own identity. When presented with the knowledge of how our identities are formed, we can take an active role in forging it ourselves.

Presently teacher professional identities do not include decision making because school structures have pushed the teacher into a nonprofessional role. As explained earlier in this book, professionals make decisions about their practices. For example, a doctor has specific procedures that must be followed as part of the profession. The doctor makes decisions about which exams should be made or which medicines to prescribe. These decisions are based on numerous factors, such as the person's previous illnesses or the kinds of medications being taken. Although doctors are accountable for their decisions, generally people do not blame doctors if their health does not improve, unless there is suspicion of malpractice. This is because healing is dependent on numerous factors, not just the skills of the doctor.

Teachers should also be considered professionals; however, they are currently treated as technicians. Technicians do not have a profession but an occupation. They do what their supervisors tell them to do. They do not make decisions but instead apply their skills as expected by the assignment. This does not fit the teaching profession because the success of teaching depends on the teacher's skills, as well as the specifics that may affect student learning. Some students learn easily; others need special approaches.

The teacher, as a professional, must make decisions based on content and pedagogical knowledge. While standards and curriculum limit what teachers do, the decisions about how to do it should be the realm of the teachers as professionals. However, this is often not the case, partly because teachers do not consider teacher agency a part of their professional identity.

Therefore, as implied by the quote at the beginning of this chapter, teachers do have a responsibility to act with agency and make decisions in their classrooms. Though school cultures often limit the decision-making power of teachers, there are ways of overcoming these limitations, as demonstrated in the account from Lileana in chapter 4.

She was an elementary school teacher in a region and a school system immersed in accountability measures. Like other school districts in the region, policies and procedures followed the overuse of top-down, mandated curricula and practices to maintain teachers' work focus on getting students to pass the state exams. As can be surmised from her account, she worked in an area with a high number of students from minority populations that included English language learners, low socioeconomic status, and other social issues normally associated with poverty and families with low levels of education.

Yet, she was able to exercise agency not within optimal conditions but in a sociocultural environment replete with factors that make teaching and learning a challenge. She did it because she had a strong identity, a strong sense of her role as an educator. To her, the most important responsibility was not to get the students to pass the state exams. Her top priority was to get her students to learn, and she believed the way to do it was to make learning fun. She made the bold choice of making learning fun at all costs because, in her heart, she believed that, while having fun, they would learn and the test results would follow. She succeeded in her task because she did all that was necessary to get her students to learn, and that is how she convinced her supervisors to allow her the agency to make decisions in her classroom, despite the fact that her practices were quite unconventional and may have appeared outlandish.

Unfortunately, many teachers have relinquished their right to make decisions to their supervisors, thinking that it is much easier to do what they are told. After all, if it does not work, they think, it is not their fault because they did what they were told. Yet, the school structures today always blame the teacher when students do not learn, so it is best to take a hold of the decision-making process with responsibility. To embrace the responsibility for making decisions, there needs to be a set of strategies that leads to success.

First and foremost, the teacher must firmly have the value for the teaching profession as something that is sacred, valuable, and important. The teacher's identity should also include an authoritative confidence in the knowledge and preparedness received from a university-based preparation program that led to a teacher certification. For those teachers who are alternatively certified, this authoritative perspective may take some time because they did not receive the benefit of a full program of preparation. Yet, the achievement of this level of authoritativeness can ultimately develop as they take the necessary steps to reach a high level of professionalism. They should reflect on their own areas of professional need and seek to overcome them through professional development that they choose for this purpose.

## Engaging in Professional Talk

The second suggestion for the appropriation of teacher agency is to engage in professional talk as a habit of mind. Teachers often use language that seems vague and unconvincing when trying to explain their practices. For example, teachers have learned that young children should engage in play as part of their development, as it will affect cognition and academic learning. Yet, when explaining why they had children playing in their prekindergarten class, teachers often make statements that seem unconvincing, such as, "The children were having some fun." This kind of statement does not explain why having fun is important or perhaps does not detail that, while playing, they were practicing their skills in self-control or following rules. The ability to speak professionally means that the teacher is fully knowledgeable of the latest research on teaching and learning, appropriate to the grade and subject they teach.

One of the reasons for Lileana's success in exercising agency was her ability to use professional language, both with her students and her professional colleagues. She taught her students to verbalize their knowledge through the use of academic language. This is why, when the superintendent walked into her class and students seemed to be playing with cookies and marshmallows, one student jumped up to explain that they were making volume cookies; he proceeded to show the superintendent how he could calculate the volume of the cookie he had made. Her use of professional language to explain her practices were also evident when she showed her principal that, through the mosaic of painted squares on her classroom floor tiles, students were engaged in calculating the perimeter of geometric shapes.

Professional talk emerges when teachers are informed about the latest approaches to teaching specific content or specific populations. As research consumers, teachers need to be aware of the conflicting research in their specific professional area. For example, there is no agreement about the best way to teach reading in the early elementary grades. While some research shows that students benefit from instruction that focuses on phonemic awareness and skills building, others show that reading instruction should focus on authentic reading in a more natural approach.

The contradictory nature of these and other findings points to the fact that teachers need to apply what is best according to the situations and the students they have. One adage that holds true in teaching is "Nothing works 100 percent of the time with 100 percent of the students." This means that the teacher needs to be a savvy research consumer, aware of the pros and cons of each method and able to articulate these ideas with the professional vocabulary and proper citation of work. This type of discourse should be part of the teacher's way of articulating professional practices and support for their decisions that go beyond trial and error or a preference based on personal taste.

## Having an Inquiry Stance

As proposed by Cochran-Smith and Lytle (2009), a teacher's ability to engage in reflective thinking has been identified as a key element in professional practice. This includes the presence of a critical stance, or the habit of questioning their own practices, their assumptions, and the assumptions inherent in all school policies and practices. One strategy for promoting this type of thinking is the use of action research that can lead to deliberate practice, as opposed to following directions or curricular approaches without analyzing and evaluating them.

Action research is a tool that undoubtedly takes the work of the teacher to a higher level for several reasons:

1. *It is based on reflective practice*. It makes use of reflection to improve practice. After teaching a lesson, teachers should evaluate which students learned and which did not. Furthermore, they should reflect on why some did not learn and what other approaches might lead to success. It is not enough to blame the lack of learning on factors

external to the class because, although there may be obstacles, the teacher's duty is to work to overcome them.
2. *It leads to proactive action.* After reflecting on situations that need to be changed, action research opens the space for the teacher to take the initiative to look for different strategies to solve the problems in instruction. They must try different techniques based on their own knowledge and research about different ways to promote academic success in specific types of students. This is why teachers use the practice of action research. They not only plan lessons with different strategies, but they also plan the collection of evidence of learning or data. Then they analyze their data to find out which techniques were successful with which students. This proactive teacher is the kind of teacher who does not merely wait for the instructions of their supervisors. They know that the best person to solve learning problems in their students is the person who is in front of the classroom. Through action research, teachers develop the ability to always base their pedagogical decisions on their own research.
3. *It raises the level of professionalism.* Finally, through action research, the teacher begins to dialogue in the professional environment in a more competent way. Through inquiry, teachers become researchers and always speak of their pedagogical practices based on the analysis of their own data, which are the results of their pedagogical practices, demonstrated through the work of their students. In this way, teachers become the authority of their practices and can intelligently discuss their pedagogical decisions, which are based on evidence.

To do this kind of research requires an inquiry stance, which means an attitude toward wanting to find solutions in logical ways and to always seek answers to the professional challenges they encounter. Action research is truly liberating for teachers because it is practitioner research, which means that teachers are not just research consumers; they are also knowledge producers.

Through action research, teachers choose to investigate better ways of teaching to address the challenges they encounter. They explore different approaches to a teaching problem, first by searching the professional literature for ways to address the teaching challenges they experience. Then they choose one or two methods to apply and collect their own data in the process. This means they collect data about their students' outcomes with the chosen approaches. Finally, through analysis of their data, teachers can modify their teaching based on the results of their practices in their own classrooms. This is a way for teachers to raise their level of professionalism, for they engage in data-based decision making instead of blindly following the curriculum guide.

## Choosing Professional Development

Once a person becomes a teacher, professional growth continues because the knowledge of learning and human development is ever evolving. For example, medical doctors must always learn about the most recent discoveries and treatments for diseases. Similarly, teacher knowledge must evolve to include the latest discoveries about learning and instructional approaches. This is why professional development is continuous, and it is usually provided in every school system based on the latest policies and needs identified at the district level.

However, the professional development provided in schools is often oriented toward the learning of specific approaches. These kinds of professional activities are important, but they should be viewed with a critical stance. Is the training being provided because large sums of money were spent on specific materials at the discretion of school administrators? Were teachers involved in these decisions about the approaches to be implemented?

Regardless of the answer to these questions, teachers should evaluate the approaches being presented as they apply to their specific students and determine possible ways to modify the lessons learned in the training, if necessary, and always with the students' best interests in mind. In addition to the enrichment activities expected by the district or school administrators, teachers must also be aware of areas they want to develop based on the specific challenges they face or the special professional areas they wish to expand. This can be done through membership in professional educational organizations or university courses that will help them to improve their professional practice.

In other words, teachers should actively engage in professional development activities suitable to their needs and wants. Most importantly, teachers should seek and choose professional activities that will help them address the challenges they face in their teaching assignments. These development activities are beyond the professional development provided by the school systems where they work.

Ideally, the self-chosen professional development includes membership in professional organizations for teachers in the specific areas of their work, such as the National Association for the Education of Young Children (NAEYC), the Council for Exceptional Children (CEC), the International Literacy Association (ILA), and the National Association of Bilingual Education (NABE).

There is an organization for different content areas or for the teaching of different kinds of student populations. These organizations provide valuable information about the best practices for each specific area. Professional development may also include obtaining higher levels of certification, such as a national board certification in a specific teaching area. National certification will lead to a higher level of professionalism, not only due to the higher level of recognition, but also due to the learning and development that is a part of the process.

**Networking for Action**

Finally, a way of engaging in professionalism that may allow for the development of teacher agency is through networking. The first kind of networking that is crucial is at the local level. Teachers cannot work in isolation, especially if they are engaging in practices that go beyond the norm in the context of their schools. Networking creates the space for dialogue and collaboration, in addition to support systems. There is strength in numbers, and explaining a new approach to solving the challenges in the classrooms is more convincing from a group of professionals than from a single unconventional teacher.

Through networking, action research can become the means of resolving challenges faced by others outside one's own classroom because often there are similarities in the kinds of teaching challenges experienced by teachers. By engaging in collaborative action research, teachers can lead their whole school toward resolving the difficulties present in their specific contexts.

Networking is also a part of the membership in professional organizations, as these not only provide knowledge about effective practices but they also offer the venue for developing professional networks and engaging in the professional community. Through these kinds of expanded networks, teachers can reach new levels of professionalism as they find new opportunities to expand the impact of their professional practices and share their knowledge.

## EMBRACING AGENCY AS A PROFESSIONAL RIGHT

In chapter 3, four components are identified as promoting the advancement of teacher agency: context, identity, positionality, and activity. The context of the profession or even of the local school setting is the most difficult to influence because it is affected by forces that are beyond the local setting. However, teachers can contribute to the development of teacher agency and make it a part of the teaching profession through their own actions, especially when they collaborate with others in this undertaking.

Teachers can contribute to the transformation of the teaching profession by consciously directing their attention to the formation of their own professional identities with the aim of positioning themselves as active agents and decision makers based on their specialized knowledge and expertise. They can also revolutionize the prototype of the teaching profession to include decision making and agency as an integral part by engaging in such activities as action research and collaboration with others through professional networks. Through these processes, teachers can lead in the creation of spaces where all teachers have the right to teach by making the professional decisions necessary for all students to succeed in learning.

*Chapter Six*

# How Can Teacher Educators and School Leaders Support Teacher Agency?

> "Human beings are not built in silence, but in word, in work, in action-reflection. . . . Consequently, no one can say a true word alone—nor can she say it for another, in a prescriptive act which robs others of their words."—Freire, 2000, p. 87

Indeed, Freire's critical pedagogy is the foundation on which our practices as educators and leaders can build teachers as professionals who are strong, critical agents who can transform education for all students in a truly democratic way. To succeed in developing teachers who have this new vision of their profession requires a transformation that arises from a critical awareness of the elements that have created the problems in education as it now exists. This transformation entails a process where teachers as learners and experts are at the center of all dialogue. This book's concluding chapter reiterates some of the theoretical constructs presented in chapter 3 and then suggests practices for school leaders and teacher educators to promote this type of agency as a central component of the teacher identity.

Within the limitations of the current public school system, at a minimum, teacher agency means that teachers can make decisions within their classrooms about how to teach their students, given the content that they are supposed to teach according to regulations. In other words, while standards and content may be mandated by state education agencies, the right to decide how to teach that content should be left to the teacher based on his or her professional preparation and the specific context of each specific classroom.

In addition to teacher agency within the classroom, this chapter also offers suggestions for promoting teacher agency collectively among teachers in a more expanded version that includes decision making to affect outcomes within schools. Thus, the application of principles requires that school principals reenvision their roles within the structure of school settings. For teacher educators, practices should promote strong professional identities and the ability to reflect at the critical level, which includes examining their practices, their assumptions, and the sociopolitical conditions that affect learning in their students.

For both school principals and teacher educators, this chapter includes specific suggestions for practices based on the same theoretical principles presented earlier that will foster the critical stance necessary for teachers to engage in agentic acts leading to quality education for all students. However, we must keep in mind Sonia Nieto's words of caution and remember, "Quick fixes never work" (2005, p. 201). They represent rigid conceptions of good practices and formulas that are transformed into packaged programs for all to follow. These do not work because every context is different. Furthermore, agency must not be imposed because an imposition cannot be considered agency at all. As suggested by the research presented in chapter 3, the teacher embraces agency once the appropriate structure and support are provided. The level of agency must be decided upon by each individual according to their preferences as members of the collective group of teachers within each school. Therefore, we must apply the principles made evident from research to guide our practices as we seek to transform the teaching profession.

The quote at the start of this chapter by Paulo Freire (2000) should serve as a guide. It includes three components: word, work, and action reflection. It means that appropriate leadership practices will open up spaces for the teachers' voices (*word*) and perspectives of their *work* and "*action-reflection*," which refers to the space where action is founded on reflection or, in other words, is data-driven through their own inquiry. Most importantly, those who are at the front, the teachers, choose the inquiry and the actions.

Given the high stakes currently in place and the vulnerability of school leaders in this process, some may ask, "Why should teachers be allowed the space to make decisions in their own classrooms or in matters that may significantly affect the way schools function?" This question needs to be paired with others, such as

- Are the schools in our nation truly promoting the highest level of education possible and facilitating the development of all students to their highest potential?
- Have we succeeded in promoting equitable education for all and significantly reduced the achievement gap?

- Are our schools stocked with highly qualified teachers who thrive in their profession?

An analysis of the current state of education in our nation reveals that the answers to these questions, in most cases, are a resounding no. For example, the Programme for International Students Assessment (PISA) developed by the Organisation for Economic Co-operation and Development (OECD) provides the answer to the first question. This assessment system examines the state of education across seventy-two countries to compare students' abilities to engage in full participation within modern societies (OECD, 2016).

The triennial two-hour survey given to more than a half-million fifteen-year-olds evaluates different kinds of knowledge and skills, including mathematics, reading, and science. In the last test, administered in 2015, Singapore ranked number 1, followed by Japan, and Estonia. Finland, a country that has ranked number 1 in the past and is recognized as a model of excellent education, was number 5. The United States was ranked number 25 on the list. These statistics reveal that we could be doing much better at promoting the highest level of education possible in our students.

If we examine the quality of education across time within our own nation by examining our own assessments of our students, we don't look any more successful. Our nation's report card as presented by the National Center for Educational Statistics (U.S. Department of Education, 2013) shows that reading and mathematics scores for students age nine, thirteen, and seventeen have not significantly changed since 1971. Although we have been somewhat successful in narrowing the achievement gap between whites, blacks, and Hispanics between 1973 and 2008, we have not continued this trend between 2008 and 2013. Results of science tests from the same agency reveal an increase in students' performance from 2008 at grades 4 and 8 but no significant change in the performance of students in grade 12.

Furthermore, the achievement gaps range between twenty-four and thirty-two points for Hispanics and thirty-four and thirty-six points for blacks. Similar gaps have also been noted for students in poverty. This means that the No Child Left Behind Act of 2001, which initiated the current system of high accountability, has not promoted a significant improvement in the quality of education nationwide in the last sixteen years, except for a few successful schools in the nation that seem to have diminished the effects of poverty on student achievement, as highlighted by Charles Payne (2017) in a recent lecture at the American Educational Research Association.

The analysis of the state of education in our nation is alarming, but so is the state of our teaching force. Though we have succeeded in maintaining the quality of teachers overall, there are two areas of significant concern:

1. teacher attrition and

2. lack of diversity in the teaching force.

Teacher attrition (Ingersoll and Collins, 2017) has been an area of concern for some time. According to the National Commission on Teaching and America's Future (NCTAF, 2016a), one-third of teachers leave the profession within the first three years of their career, and half leave the profession within five years. This is an alarming trend because teaching is a complex profession that requires years of experience to promote high-quality practices.

A study done by Farber (2010), a teacher and educational leader, shows that teachers' reasons for leaving the profession include low pay, increased responsibilities, excessive bureaucracy, and, of course, the negative effects of high-stakes testing on school climate, curriculum, teaching schedules, and students' well-being, among other things. If teachers leave the profession in large numbers, then we can deduce that they never reach their maximum potential in their ability to teach, and they are certainly not thriving. NCTAF's recommendation, in their report *What Matters Now: A New Compact for Teaching and Learning* (NCTAF, 2016b), is a transformation in the way schools function, which includes placing teachers at the heart of the system by giving them opportunities for choice in professional development and engagement in school leadership. This is a call for teacher agency.

In addition to the concerns over teacher attrition, the lack of diversity in the teaching force has also been emphasized. This lack of representation among teachers from different racial and ethnic backgrounds, as well as a lack of teachers who are male, especially black males, is alarming. According to a report by the U.S. Department of Education (2016), studies have shown that racial diversity among teachers can be beneficial for students. Diverse teachers come with a high degree of cultural competence and can provide culturally sensitive teaching practices to those who most need it, which may reduce the achievement gap.

As stated in the report, teachers of color provide good role models who dispel negative stereotypes of minorities, are more likely to have high expectations for all students, and are more likely to refer students of color to gifted programs. Many of them are more familiar with the communities surrounding the school. Yet, the disparity between student–teacher diversity is alarming. The report expects that, by 2024, 56 percent of the student population will comprise students of color, yet today, 82 percent of the teaching force in the United States is white. Because this figure has not significantly changed in fifteen years, a major change in the years ahead is unforeseeable.

A call for diversity in the teaching force should not imply that white teachers are less valued. On the contrary, there are many white teachers who are committed to the success of all their students regardless of their diverse backgrounds, their social economic status, or special learning needs, as explained by Sonia Nieto (2005) in her book *Why We Teach*. Nevertheless, in our search for social justice, a more diverse teaching force should be viewed as an outcome of an equitable society.

The strong call in this book for the teachers' voice in the educational dialogue and decision-making processes within their classrooms and schools must include the diverse perspectives of those who experience education from a place of disadvantage. These include the English language learners who experienced bilingual education as children, and the blacks who experienced segregation or racial prejudice as students, as well as other diverse groups who can bring perspectives into the dialogue that we are not yet aware of. These voices are of particular significance because they represent the voices of the few who were able to overcome school-based obstacles, and they can provide insightful knowledge from a different perspective not shared by their colleagues who are white. It is in this rich kind of diversity that teacher agency can promote social justice in a most efficacious way.

From the data presented here, the state of education is not optimal. We are not providing the best possible education for all of our nation's students, education is not equitable, and students are not thriving in our schools despite all our efforts. The one element we have not considered thus far is to ask teachers what can be done to improve learning in the classroom. This is why teacher agency is presented here as the most logical solution.

## KEY PRINCIPLES TO BE APPLIED

Chapter 3 presents a comprehensive discussion with support from research about learning principles that can serve as a foundation to promote the professional development of teachers so they can engage in teacher agency. The theoretical constructs that can be applied for a transformation of the teacher as a professional are the cultural-historical theory of learning, adult learning theory, and critical pedagogy.

The application of these three theoretical frameworks combined should lead to practices where learning and development include collaboration at all levels and where the teachers as learners actively coproduce knowledge. Cultural-historical principles focus on the value of interaction and social learning. This means that

- professional development activities and the evolution of working practices within a school are led by the teachers and instructional leaders together;
- teachers' collective work scaffolds the learning of new instructional methods or ways of being professional, which in turn are interpreted by each individual, who learns to engage actively in the social context of the working environment;

- collectively, teachers in the school interpret their evolving understandings of learning and work in their classrooms;
- collectively, teachers engage in practitioner inquiry and transform their practices as they find solutions to the problems encountered, based on analysis of their own data; and
- school transformation is the result of goals, objectives, and actions developed by the collective group of teachers with their school leaders.

These suggestions are also in harmony with adult learning theory and critical pedagogy. To promote transformations, adult learning theory stresses the importance of critical reflection, which validates the use of the collaborative practices suggested here, as well as the implementation of inquiry. They are most appropriate in the creation of spaces for critical reflection, especially critical reflection of assumptions and meaning perspectives emphasized by Mezirow (1998).

Additionally, critical pedagogy is applied through the process of collective work when teachers are encouraged to examine the sociopolitical forces that affect the context of their work, for it represents the action-reflection implied by Freire in the citation at the beginning of this chapter. Freire's statement subsumes reflections and actions that include the elements affecting learning, such as cognitive and emotional development, as well as the sociopolitical aspects that infringe on social justice. Notice in the quote by Freire (2000) that the process should not be a *"prescriptive act which robs others of their words"* (p. 87). In this case, it would rob teachers of their right to exercise agency in their professional acts.

## CREATING SPACES FOR TEACHER AGENCY IN SCHOOLS

The transformation of the work for the promotion of teacher agency can be achieved through evolving stages. There are two levels for promoting teacher agency in schools. First, teachers can be allowed some level of agency within their own classrooms, as exemplified by Lileana in chapter 4, when she states that the administrators had to be supportive and allow her to be creative and make decisions about her teaching practices. The second level for promoting teacher agency is more comprehensive. Teachers can be allowed to exercise agency by collectively engaging in making decisions.

It is important to keep in mind that no specific models or prepackaged solutions can be provided. The suggestions presented here are based on principles of human development, where the best model is the one that emerges from the work and interactions with teachers who are valued as professionals and not as technicians who can follow a formula. Thus, the space created for teacher agency should allow for dialogue and collaboration with the instructional leaders, where the teachers are the creators of their own professional practice to achieve the best results when working with their students.

Also, the evaluation of their work should not be based on the minimalist measures created by school-accountability policies but by the achievement of goals created by them in collaboration with the school administrators for the benefit of all students. So, success should be measured not only by the results on tests but also by the quality of the overall education, which includes those measured by standardized tests *and* measures of students' overall intellectual and emotional development and their ability to critically analyze different kinds of content beyond those measured by the state exams.

The students' understandings should include social studies, art, music, health, and writing, as well as reading, math, and science. The evaluation of teachers should be based on their abilities to help each child succeed and reach their full potential. Though a complicated process, this view of learning must be the goal of education in America if we are to promote a democratic society—a society where everyone is valued and everyone receives quality education, not just the few who are most fortunate because of their socioeconomic status.

## Teacher Agency within Classrooms

At a minimal level, teacher agency should be encouraged within classrooms. In other words, though expected to cover the content of each discipline as mandated by policies that usually adhere to standards of knowledge and skills to be taught at each specific grade level, teachers should be allowed to make decisions about how to organize their classroom routines and the ways to teach their lessons.

Lileana provides an example of this in chapter 4, even though she worked in a school that was traditional and did not include an environment where teachers normally made professional decisions. In this case, Lileana was able to engage in teacher agency because she considered it part of her professional identity. She positioned herself in a way that allowed her to do it successfully, but she was also allowed to engage in agentic acts by her principal, who, though hesitantly at first, allowed her to exercise teacher agency as she planned and implemented her lessons and workshops. Though creative and unorthodox in her approach, her success led her principal to assign her a position of leadership. In her second year of teaching as the mathematics leader in her elementary school, she was asked to share her approaches with others so they, too, could succeed.

Teachers who find ways to engage in professionalism as self-initiators of their practices often are chastised for not complying with the top-down decisions about curriculum practices, while others are allowed to share their success, depending on the philosophy followed by the school principal. In the current educational context, most principals seem to veer toward a more controlling approach that limits agency for teachers and a lack of trust.

Permitting the teachers decision-making power within the classroom offers some possibilities. Teachers can make use of their knowledge to promote lessons that will lead to success. However, allowing this level of agency requires support that may include additional professional development based on the challenges identified by the teacher in collaboration with school leaders. Note that the suggestion here is not for specific methods to be determined in a top-down fashion but for the teacher to identify the challenges and the areas he or she deems appropriate to increase development and lead to success. Teachers need to have a voice in choosing their professional development in ways that will lead to their success, as is recommended by NCTAF (2016b) in their report *What Matters Now*.

In many schools, it is a general understanding that teachers are free to make pedagogical decisions, yet true autonomy is not often the case. For example, in some schools, the supervising staff articulate openness in decision making, yet there are often mandates that come directly from the district office to implement specific types of programs, such as RTI, weekly fluency tests, TELPAS assessments, preparation for the high-stakes tests, accelerated school projects, and reading renaissance, to name a few. There are also professional development practices where teachers are mandated to apply what was learned. In some schools, frequent, unexpected schedule changes or events make previously planned activities and lessons completely impossible to implement.

In addition, the curriculum materials presented to teachers are predetermined in a top-down fashion without teachers' input, and these are often expected to be used in way that limits modifications needed to meet the needs of specific students. Alternative approaches are often not allowed. It is important to provide support for teachers so their professional practices are continuously developed. As the practitioners in the front lines, they are in the best position to make decisions about the specific areas of development in their students based on the challenges present in their classrooms.

A good way of opening up spaces for professional decision making may include the promotion of data-based decision making through teacher-practitioner research, often called action research. In this approach, teachers are asked to investigate ways to improve student outcomes by collecting their own data on different techniques used and then reflecting on the results of their efforts. The purpose is to promote practices that are based on their own practitioner research within their classrooms based on specific challenges they choose to investigate. Action research has been a part of the professional discourse in preservice and in-service teacher development internationally for more than twenty years (Cochran-Smith, 1992; Cochran-Smith and Lytle, 2009; McNiff, 2013; Mertler, 2016; Ostorga and Estrada, 2009), yet it has not become the norm in the teaching profession. Given the benefits of inquiry-based practices, it is important to promote its use at all levels.

## Teacher Agency as a Collective Activity in Schools

The creation of spaces for teacher decision making within their own classrooms has its limitations. Teachers are isolated, and the practices across different classrooms of the same grade are so varied, leading to different results and different learning. School administrators have a need to find some level of standardization so that the quality of instruction is somewhat similar across the different classrooms. Though standardization is often favored, the fact that each classroom is made up of significantly different kinds of students with different needs and abilities does not usually enter into the analysis when the desire is to achieve equal results; this does not account for the unevenness of human nature.

A much more effective approach is to promote teacher agency as a collective part of the educational community in a school. For this to occur, there are some important factors to consider. Undoubtedly, as teacher agency is presented for consideration, many school leaders may connect the concept to the current movement for teacher leadership. Although teacher leadership and teacher agency may seem like similar concepts, there are important considerations.

For many, teacher leadership is a role assigned to a select number of effective teachers, who are eventually moved out of the classroom. For these folks, the hidden assumption is that there is more value in administrative leadership roles than in teaching. For that reason, teacher leaders often have extra merit pay because they have more responsibilities. Yet, a different definition of teacher leadership comes from the educators in the Whole Child Initiative of the Association for Supervision and Curriculum Development (ASCD, 2015). This initiative focuses the dialogue about educational improvement away from the narrow view on academic achievement to a broader view of deep, long-lasting learning spanning all subject areas, not just those assessed by standardized tests.

During a Whole Child Symposium in 2014 sponsored by ASCD, educators engaged in an analysis of teacher leadership as an important component in school improvement. According to their definition of the term, leadership is an integral part of the profession, and all teachers must be prepared and mentored to become leaders, each in their own way. In other words, teacher leadership should become an expectation of the profession, a part of the school culture, and all teachers should have an opportunity, in their own way, to be leaders.

Teacher leadership should be promoted because it has been associated with higher levels of student engagement, as explained by Leithwood and

Jantzi (2006) in their study of a large-scale reform in England schools, in the late 1990s. Furthermore, they go on to say that, given the complexities in today's schools, the responsibility for student learning must be a collaborative effort and cannot be accomplished without teacher leadership.

Yet, while teacher leadership is an important part of the teaching profession, we should not force all teachers to become leaders, and it is not advisable to think that teacher agency should be reserved for those capable of becoming leaders in their profession. Crucial in this process is to allow teachers to create themselves rather than imposing a prepackaged trait on everyone. Thus, agency is a part of teacher leadership and should be considered part of the teacher's professional mode of work.

The eventual goal should be to create a community of practice (Lave and Wenger, 1991; Wenger, McDermott, and Snyder, 2002), where agency emerges from dialogue and the flow of ideas. The focus should be placed on creating an environment of trust and creativity with clear purposes and values while encouraging innovation. This means that every teacher should be given the tools to be able to get into their profession and to work with others so they can expand their own practice and the professional practice of others in their realm. When the teaching profession evolves so that this level of work is the expectation, then we will have teacher agency as part of the profession.

How can this level of leadership be facilitated so that agency becomes an integral part of the teaching profession? The answer to this question can be found in the work of Hargreaves and Fink (2005) in their book *Sustainable Leadership*. In this book, the authors outline seven principles for sustainable leadership. It is a way to advance innovations in schools, which promote positive changes that last beyond the presence of the leader who initiated them.

Of special significance in our discussion about ways to promote teacher agency is the third principle presented in the framework, called breadth. It refers to the idea that leadership should flow throughout an organization rather than in a hierarchical direction. First introduced in the 1960s, this principle is based on the idea that, when organizational decisions are shared, people naturally work toward the common goals developed by all, without the need for tight controls and excessive supervision.

Hargreaves and Fink (2005) present numerous studies that have demonstrated the positive effects of this type of leadership on student learning. As well as positive outcomes in teacher morale and effectiveness, the most astonishing explanation about distributed leadership revealed in their book is that, in reality, whether planned or not, it is everywhere inside and outside of schools, in and out of the classrooms, during school or after school, in the teacher's lounge, in the lunchroom, between classes, and on weekends. This is because humans by nature are free agents. Thus, when the principal aims to control their actions, they may comply but will always find ways to reinterpret the directions and to infuse their values and beliefs into their practices.

Teacher agency is always present, but this kind of agency does not lead to fruitful results for all because it is a way to preserve one's own individuality. Furthermore, a limit on a teacher's ability to engage in agentic professional actions may very well be a reason for leaving the profession. The positive benefits of distributed leadership are also documented by Spillane (2012).

For other teachers, whose professional identity include a vision for sharing their knowledge to the profession at large, engaging in professional agency outside the classroom may lead them to promote transformation in the profession while they remain in the teaching profession. These types of teachers are rare, but they show us the possibilities of what being a true professional teacher can mean: one whose work spans across different professional circles.

A most notable example of this type of leadership is Dr. Rebecca Palacios, retired kindergarten teacher of thirty-four years, who was one of the founders of the National Board for Professional Teaching Standards (NBPTS), a national certification organization for teachers in the United States. Even after receiving her doctorate degree and while serving as the vice president of this organization, she continued teaching kindergarten until her retirement. Her work significantly affected the teaching profession in positive ways. Another example is Katie Farber, a teacher and engaged professional who is active in promoting positive transformations beyond the classroom. As an author and blogger, she is recognized for her many contributions to the profession.

These are examples of teachers who refused to be limited by the constraints placed on them by school structures. Given their creativity and insight imparted to the educational community, one can only imagine the kinds of actions these teachers engaged in that led to positive impact on their students. Their acts represent self-initiated leadership outside of their classrooms or schools, independent of the leadership style of their principals.

Some fear that allowing teachers the freedom to make the decisions can lead to chaos. These fears are based on assumptions that teachers are lazy and will act unethically. The same can be said of principals and district administrators. Sure, due to human nature, undoubtedly there are many professionals who are unethical; that is why they must be held accountable for their actions. Yet limiting their ability to apply their knowledge and expertise is not the best way to promote ethical practices, for top-down, predetermined procedures do not work in the messy and complex context of everyday life in classrooms.

The neat scripts provided by expensive curriculum packages and instructional models fall apart when implemented in classrooms with students who have diverse needs and abilities. No matter how perfect the prepackaged, research-based models seem to be, they always need to be adapted in real, live classrooms, when intervening variables get in the way, and no one is more adept at doing this than a well-qualified, experienced teacher.

Thus, teachers need to be given the space to adapt those carefully designed procedures because of the human factor present in the teaching profession. Unexpected leadership emerges in the classrooms of conscientious teachers who hold their students' development and well-being as the top priority, even at the possible expense of losing their jobs. This is made evident in chapter 4 by Lileana, when she was willing to take risks so her students would benefit.

Like her, others may express agency, when not watched perhaps, and apply their expertise or intuition to address the challenges that emerge in practice. Yet, in these situations, the positive effects of the practice are often shortchanged by the many limitations created by top-down procedural regulations, and these practices cannot always be maximized for the benefit of students because they are not systematized. When left to chance, high-quality practices may be implemented only when possible, for some and not others, depending on the circumstances.

Though performed with the best intentions in mind, these actions are examples of distributed leadership that is unplanned. These leadership opportunities can be positive or negative. The results are haphazard rather than carefully orchestrated. There are also examples of teacher agency or unplanned, distributed leadership that is negative, the result of anger and deceit precisely because teachers feel diminished and devalued as professionals. Therefore, promoting planned distributed leadership that leads to the most beneficial outcomes is challenging, especially when it is first implemented in the more traditional schools or with young, transient staff.

A progressive scale of leadership distribution can be most beneficial (Hargreaves and Fink, 2006, p. 138). Principals can begin the process through progressive delegation by setting up special committees and assigning specific leadership roles to teachers who are most ready for these types of leadership.

Another approach to creating spaces for agency can be found in principles for creating in schools communities of practice (COP) (Lave and Wenger, 1991; Wenger, 1998). In this approach, the teachers as a collective group engage in the planning of goals for the school, along with ways to resolve the challenges and achieve these goals. Within the schoolwide community of teachers, there should also be spaces for subgroups to work on challenges that are specific to their classroom contexts, such as the specific challenges related to their grades or content areas or students' special needs and abilities, cultures, or lives. These are some of the practices that can be implemented by school leaders to promote agency as part of the teaching profession and hold teachers accountable for positive transformations in the school that are appropriate to the local context.

The validity of teacher agency and the essentiality of collaboration in this process of school improvement can be inferred from a study about teacher ownership conducted by the Annenberg Institute for School Reform. This national policy-research and reform support organization housed at Brown University has carried out numerous studies to inform the improvement of schools. The concept of teacher ownership is intimately connected to teacher agency and is defined as *"a teacher's sense of alignment with an improvement effort and agency to influence it"* (Saunders et al., 2017, p. 1). This is aligned with the findings of the case study conducted by Farris-Berg, Dirkswager, and Junge (2012) and presented in their book *Trusting Teachers with School Success: What Happens When Teacher Calls the Shots*.

Teacher ownership evolves from practices that allow teachers to build a system of coherence as they engage in solving problems collectively. It is an essential element in successful school transformations. The school improvement that results from collective efforts places teachers at the center of the school reform as coconstructors of positive, systemic change. This process is built on collaboration, as teachers collectively define their school. The evaluation of their work focuses on the elements of shared practices, which build collective capacity for transformations.

## THE PREPARATION OF TEACHERS FOR TEACHER AGENCY

In the current context of education, we at university-based teacher-preparation programs prepare teachers to reflect critically and to engage in inquiry so their decisions are informed by data. Yet, once our preservice teachers graduate, they are given strict directions about what and how to teach and are usually not given the space to engage in reflective practices or practitioner research. They are stripped of their right to make informed decisions based on the specific needs of the students in their classrooms.

Indeed, the punitive measures imposed by school administrators due to accountability (Ravitch, 2010) not only strips teachers of their professional rights, but it also scares them into submitting to the demands placed on them by their supervisors and shortchanges their students out of a high-quality education. The emphasis on scripted curricula and school-mandated teaching methods is generally present in school systems across the United States but is more prevalent in schools that serve low-socioeconomic communities (Orfield and Lee, 2005). Furthermore, the teacher, a professional educated on the best practices to promote learning, is generally left out of the dialogue about educational reform and the best ways to educate children throughout the world (Villegas-Reimers and Reimers, 1996; Weber, 2007).

This book begins with a discussion about the need for teacher agency. In the introduction, two assumptions about the teaching profession are identified as crucial to its development. One relates to the social view of the profession. Teaching must be valued and respected as a complex profession, similar to the medical and law professions. This view of teaching depends on many variables that are not easily manipulated. However, we can consciously work toward the second assumption; we can promote the teacher's authoritative confidence and awareness of his or her preparedness to consider the profession one of high value and worthy of pride, to "take a proactive stance toward the education of all of our children" (Flessner et al., 2012, p. xvii).

This last section is primarily directed toward teacher educators, though its contents can also be useful to school principals. Based on the current educational contexts, how can teacher educators best prepare teachers to engage in teacher agency and to take charge of their professional practices? How can we teach them to lead their students to success by applying what they learn in the pre- and in-service phases? The research and theoretical principles presented in chapter 3 have implications for teacher preparation. Four elements are presented here as essential to this process:

1. activism as part of the professional identity (Freire, 2013);
2. engagement in critical reflection (Brookfield, 2017; King and Kitchener, 2004; Mezirow, 1998);
3. an inquiry stance (Cochran-Smith and Lytle, 2009; Edwards, 2007); and
4. participation in collaborative professional discourse (Lave and Wenger, 1991; Farris-Berg, Dirkswager, and Junge, 2012).

Some of these elements have already been a part of the professional dialogue about teacher preparation; however, they are presented here in ways that make it specific to the development of teacher agency. They are all fundamental in the development of a transformed professional identity that includes agency as a right to be exercised. In chapter 1 of this book, I suggest the following two principles necessary to transform the teaching profession so that teachers can become professionals:

1. Initiate efforts to bring highly capable individuals into the teaching profession.
2. Give teachers a central role in the dialogue about school reform and policies.

It is obvious that the transformation being called for requires efforts on different levels, from teacher educators, school leaders, and policy makers. Here we focus on what teacher educators can do to promote this transformation, which begins with the first step outlined here, to ensure that candidates are highly capable.

We already know the goal for the preparation of teachers includes coursework and activities that provide them with the knowledge of the content they will teach, as well as pedagogical knowledge and pedagogical content knowledge. It further includes the development of a set of proper dispositions for the profession, which have refined over the years (Murrell et al., 2010). University-based teacher-preparation programs have already addressed these needs. However, there is one more area to be included here: activism.

## Activism as Part of the Professional Identity

Activism is not a disposition normally included in the goals of teacher preparation. Perhaps a disposition that approximates activism is advocacy, yet activism goes beyond advocacy because, in addition to supporting a cause, it includes action that is direct and purposeful. A prerequisite for the attitude of activism is a process of conscientization, for it fosters a critical stance and makes teachers ready to become advocates and activists.

To foster conscientization, the educator must find ways to help future teachers learn to trust their own knowledge and experiences. As Joan Wink (2000) explains, teachers are powerful human beings who can have a positive impact on the lives of their students, yet they are fearful of making decisions because the educational system pushes them into a passive role, leading them to see themselves as victims (p. 37). So, teacher educators must find ways to help future teachers become strong and aware of the value of their professional knowledge.

In other words, teachers must develop a habit of mind where they critically examine the knowledge they have and their actions. This process must include the courage and ability to question their knowledge and practices, as well as the knowledge of others. Teachers need to examine how their actions are sometimes promoting the same negative outcomes they seek to transform, and they must have the courage to change ways of teaching that are not working, even if it does not match the directions they receive.

Then they need the courage to explain why their actions are different from what is demanded by their supervisors, as Lileana did in her class (see chapter 4). Additionally, they must go beyond the critical examination of their actions and results, for they should also be ready to critically scrutinize and question the accepted knowledge, which is the laws, structures, and practices of school, as well as the research and curriculum that is accepted as the norm.

As explained by Dover, Henning, and Agarwal-Rangnath (2016), neoliberal mandates and privatization of assessments for students, teachers, and teacher educators have a deprofessionalizing and disempowering impact on teachers, and are undermining the integrity of the teacher-preparation process, leading teachers to see themselves as accountable to external authorities rather than the priorities of the students in their classrooms. We teacher educators must facilitate in teachers the development of agency as part of their professional identity so they can find strategic ways to engage in their practices amid the restrictive mandates. They must understand that they can use their right to think and act for themselves in a way that embodies a vision of practices for social justice. This can be accomplished through critical compliance and reflective resistance based on critical reflection.

## Engagement in Critical Reflection

Critical thinking has been an integral part of teacher preparation, usually referred to as critical reflection. Yet the definition of *critical reflection* is not always clear, and many educators think of it as the ability to examine one's practice. In reality, critical reflection goes beyond evaluation of practice to include one's assumptions and meaning perspectives, as explained by Mezirow (1998).

Critical thinking, or reflection, is key in the development of teachers for many reasons. First, research has shown that teacher beliefs inform their practices more than preparation or training (Murrell et al., 2010), yet beliefs are formed early in life (Lortie, 2002) through cultural transmission, and these beliefs and values filter the interpretations of realities or new learning (Pajares, 1992). They are not easily changed, which is why simplistic forms of training do not work. Chapter 3 presents a detailed explanation of adult learning principles and what is required for transformation of meaning perspectives and value systems. Because belief systems are culturally transmitted, then it is through collective practices that transformation can occur.

The answer lies in the application of learning principles that will lead to transformation of their assumptions or perspectives. As explained by Mezirow (1990),

> perspective transformation is the process of becoming critically aware of how and why our assumptions have come to constrain the way we perceive, understand, and feel about the world; changing the structures of habitual expectations to make possible a more inclusive, discriminating, and integrating perspective; and, finally, making choices or otherwise acting upon these new understandings. (p. 14)

How do we engage teachers in becoming aware of their beliefs? How do we teach critical thinking? First, we must become critical pedagogues ourselves. Proponents of critical pedagogy argue that "school practices are designed to maintain and sustain the status quo by reinforcing white supremacy, maintaining patriarchy, and promoting capitalist values" (Generett, 2009, p. 83).

Therefore, teacher educators must apply what is called engaged pedagogy to transform themselves and to lead their future teachers on a journey of self-transformation by helping them become aware of the hegemonic practices that have affected and will be present everywhere when as they enter the teaching profession. Only after the awareness emerges, only after the process of conscientization, can teacher educators lead these future teachers to engage in their own inquiry about theories and practices in what is called practitioner research.

Moreover, the conscientization process requires that the relationship between the teacher educator and the future teachers be collaborative and dialogical. Preservice teachers need to not only be exposed to theory and research; they must also be exposed to the many contradictions and the debates in the education field. Although educators tend to favor particular philosophies and approaches, they must present theory and research from diverse perspectives and engage students in critical explorations of the pedagogical content. Subsequently, they will become intelligent users of research and creators of their own knowledge as it applies to the specific contexts of the classrooms they experience. Instead of sheltering them from debates so we can further our own views, they must be exposed to the controversies of their future profession such as:

- Teach the parts and skills first (phonemic awareness), or engage students in a whole-language approach (reading a story) and then zero in on the detailed skills?
- Focus instruction on just the core standards mandated by state policies, or enrich instruction with knowledge that goes beyond the mandated standards?
- Allow limited-English-proficient students to interact with their peers in their first language to facilitate the learning of the content in a bilingual classroom, or discourage the use of the first language at all costs?

These are just a few of the current debates in education. If we want our students of teaching to exercise agency in their profession, then we must begin early to create the space where they can explore different perspectives and critically examine the issues as they apply to the individual students they encounter in their field experiences. Then they must begin by being allowed to exercise agency in controlled and ever-expanding ways during their coursework at the preservice phase. The knowledge that emerges from this process is complex and will be composed of different perspectives, and for some, it will not match the knowledge assessed in certification exams because some preservice teachers will develop perspectives and philosophies that do not match those considered valid by the policy makers and the creators of certification exams.

Accordingly, given that we teacher educators are held accountable for the knowledge our students receive, we must also help them understand how their perspectives relate to the accepted knowledge and help them understand how to critically view the certification exams they must successfully complete. This means that we teacher educators must teach future teachers to differentiate between their own pedagogical perspectives and the perspectives of others who evaluate their knowledge. This knowledge will help them in their journey toward agency.

## An Inquiry Stance

Another integral part of teacher development should be the use of inquiry or practitioner research. The process of inquiry after conscientization is a way to transform the self-creation of their professional identities. Only if teachers learn how to navigate the controversial and hegemonic realities of education can they learn to make professional decisions without suffering adverse consequences. Practitioner research is a tool to help them in this process, for they can make use of data and analysis to substantiate their practices and give them the appropriate language to dialogue as professionals within their work environment.

Again, it is crucial to maintain a dialogic approach when engaging future teachers in action research by creating a democratic environment and spaces for critical discussions within coursework instead of lecture-based approaches that place the college students, future teachers, as passive receivers of knowledge from the teacher educators. Action research is an opportune way of engaging future teachers in the practices of undergraduate research and is currently being proposed in many colleges and universities.

## Participation in Collaborative Professional Discourse

Finally, it is imperative that teachers who are decision makers and activists be adept in creating and maintaining collaborative networks. This development begins in the preservice phase as they engage in critical dialogues with their mentor teachers in the field, as well as with their peers. Properly orchestrated activities, such as team assignments, can teach them to engage with professionals in intelligent dialogue.

A way of promoting collaborative professional discourse is through the use of action research assignments that are related to the teacher educator's own areas of research. Through these practices, future teachers become a part of a collaborative team engaging in crucial issues in the field of education appropriate to their contexts.

Finally, engaging future teachers in collaborative discourse in this manner allows for the integration of all four essential elements in teacher preparation.

The development of skills for professional collaboration is essential for their work as activists because the goals of systemic transformation can only be achieved through collaborative networks. Likewise, critical reflection and practitioner research function in harmony with collaborative discourse, for it creates a social context in which both of these practices can thrive and lead to continuous improvement of professional practices.

## FINAL WORDS

This chapter closes this book about the development of teacher agency, which includes theoretical frameworks and their applications to foster strong professional identities. The ability to engage in the teaching profession with agency requires efforts at multiple levels, beginning with the teachers in the classrooms, but also connecting to all the related components of the school systems, which include the school leaders, the teacher educators, and the policy makers.

Through the research carried out by the Annenberg Institute for School Reform (Saunders et al., 2017), we learn that teacher ownership is a key element in the promotion of reforms that will lead to positive changes. This means that teachers cannot be viewed just as implementers of new programs, but they also must have the commitment to change, which can come when they have a voice in its creation and implementation. This requires the space where they can exercise their right to make decisions, or their right to engage in practices based on their knowledge and expertise—their right to teach.

# References

Alicea, V. G. (1990). Introduction. *Journal of Educational Facilitation* 1 (1): 1–3.
Anfara, V. A., Brown, K. M., & Mangione, T. L. (2002). Qualitative analysis on stage: Making the research process more public. *Educational Researcher* 31 (7): 28–38. https://doi.org/10.3102/0013189X031007028.
Angus, D. L. (2001, January). Professionalism and the public good: A brief history of teacher certification. J. Mirel (Ed.). *Thomas D. Fordham Foundation*. https://edex.s3-us-west-2.amazonaws.com/publication/pdfs/angus_7.pdf.
Arce, J., Luna, D., Borjian, A., & Conrad, M. (2005). No child left behind: Who wins? Who loses? *Social Justice*, 32(3[101]), 56–71. Retrieved from http://www.jstor.org/stable/29768321
Association for Supervision and Curriculum Development (2015). Teacher leadership: The what, why and how of teacher leaders. ASCD Whole Child Symposium, fall 2014, Alexandria, VA.
Beijaard, D., Meijer, P. C., & Verloop, N. (2004). Reconsidering research on teachers' professional identity. *Teaching and Teacher Education* 20 (2): 107–28.
Biddle, B. J., & Berliner, D. C. (2002). Unequal school funding in the United States. *Educational Leadership* 59 (8): 48–59.
Biesta, G., & Tedder, M. (2007). Agency and learning in the life course: Towards an ecological perspective. *Studies in Education of Adults* 39: 132–49.
Braun, H. I. (2005). Using student progress to evaluate teachers: A primer on value-added models. Policy information perspective. *Educational Testing Service*. https://eric.ed.gov/?id=ED529977.
Brookfield, S. D. (2017). *Becoming a critically reflective teacher*. 2nd ed. San Francisco: Jossey-Bass.
Brown, E. (2015, April 14). Nine Atlanta educators in test-cheating case are sentenced to prison. *Washington Post*. https://www.washingtonpost.com/local/education/eight-atlanta-educators-in-test-cheating-case-sentenced-to-prison/2015/04/14/08a9d26e-e2bc-11e4-b510-962fcfabc310_story.html.
Bush, R.N. (1984). Effective staff development in *Making schools more effective: Proceedings of three state conferences*. West Lab for Educational Research and Development, San Francisco, CA.
Center for Education Policy. (2008, February). Instructional time in elementary schools: A closer look at changes for specific subjects. A report in the series From the Capital to the Classroom: Year 5 of the No Child Left Behind Act, Washington, DC.
Chilcott, L., & Guggenheim, D. (2010). *Waiting for Superman*. Paramount Vantage.

Clandinin, D. J., Long, J., Schaefer, L., Downey, C. A., Steeves, P., Pinnegar, E., Robblee, S. M., & Wnuk, S. (2015). Early career teacher attrition: Intentions of teachers beginning. *Teaching Education* 26 (1): 1–16. https://doi.org/10.1080/10476210.2014.996746.

Cochran-Smith, M. (1992). *Inside/outside: Teacher research and knowledge.* S. L. Lytle (Ed.). New York: Teachers College Press.

Cochran-Smith, M., & Lytle, S. L. (2009). *Inquiry as stance: Practitioner research for the next generation.* New York: Teachers College Press.

Cohn, M. M. (1992). *Teachers: The missing voice in education.* Albany: State University of New York Press.

Cole, M., Engeström, Y., & Vasquez, O. (1997). *Mind culture and activity: Seminal papers from the laboratory of comparative human cognition.* Cambridge: Cambridge University Press.

Cubberley, E. P. (1947). *Public education in the United States: A study and interpretation of American educational history.* Boston: Houghton Mifflin. http://archive.org/details/publiceducationi032029mbp.

Davies, B., & Harré, R. (1999). "Positioning and personhood." In R. Harré & L. van Langenhove (Eds.), *Positioning theory: Moral contexts of international action* (pp. 32–52). Oxford, UK: Wiley-Blackwell.

Dee, T. S., & Jacob, B. A. (2010). The impact of no child left behind on students, teachers, and schools. *Brookings Papers on Economic Activity* 2: 149–94. https://doi.org/10.1353/eca.2010.0014.

Dover, A. G., Henning, N., & Agarwal-Rangnath, R. (2016). Reclaiming agency: Justice-oriented social studies teachers respond to changing curricular standards. *Teaching and Teacher Education* 59: 457–67.

Edwards, A. (2007). Relational agency in professional practice: A CHAT analysis. *Action: An International Journal of Human Activity Theory* 1: 1–17.

Enyedy, N., Goldberg, J., & Welsh, K. M. (2006). Complex dilemmas of identity and practice. *Science Education, 90*(1), 68–93. https://doi.org/10.1002/sce.20096

Farber, K. (2010). *Why teachers quit: And how we might stop the exodus.* Thousand Oaks, CA: Corwin.

Farris-Berg, K., Dirkswager, E. J., & Junge, A. (2012). *Trusting teachers with school success: What happens when teachers call the shots.* Lanham, MD: Rowman and Littlefield Education.

Flessner, R., Miller, G., Patrizio, K., & Horwitz, J. (2012). *Agency through teacher education: Reflection, community, and learning.* Lanham, MD: Rowman and Littlefield.

Flores, M. A., & Day, C. (2006). Contexts which shape and reshape new teachers' identities: A multi-perspective study. *Teaching and Teacher Education* 22 (2): 219–32. https://doi.org/10.1016/j.tate.2005.09.002.

Freire, P. (2000). *Pedagogy of the oppressed.* 30th anniversary ed. New York: Bloomsbury Academic.

Freire, P. (2013). *Education for critical consciousness.* Reprint ed. London: Bloomsbury Academic.

Gamson, D. A., Lu, X., & Eckert, S. A. (2013). Challenging the research base of the common core state standards: A historical reanalysis of text complexity. *Educational Researcher* 42 (7): 381–91. http://doi.org/10.3102/0013189X13505684.

Generett, G. G. (2009). "Engaging bell hooks: How teacher educators can work to sustain themselves and their work." In M. D. Davidson & G. Yancy (Eds.), *Critical Perspectives on bell hooks.* New York: Routledge.

Goldhaber, D., & Cowan, J. (2014). Excavating the teacher pipeline: Teacher preparation programs and teacher attrition. *Journal of Teacher Education* 65 (5): 449–62. https://doi.org/10.1177/0022487114542516.

Goldstein, D. (2015). *The teacher wars: A history of America's most embattled profession.* New York: Anchor.

Goldstein, L. (1999). The relational zone: The role of caring relationships in the co-construction of mind. *American Educational Research Journal* 36 (3): 647–73.

# References

Haapasaari, A., Engeström, Y., & Kerouso, H. (2016). The emergence of learners' transformative agency in a change laboratory intervention. *Journal of Education and Work* 29 (2): 232–62. https://doi.org/10.1080/13639080.2014.900168.

Hargreaves, A., & Fink, D. (2005). *Sustainable leadership*. 1st ed. San Francisco: Jossey-Bass.

Hodge, S. (2011). Learning to manage: Transformative outcomes of competency-based training. *Australian Journal of Adult Learning* 51 (3): 498–517.

Hoffman, N. (2003). *Woman's "true" profession: Voices from the history of teaching*. 2nd ed. Cambridge, MA: Harvard Education Press.

Ingersoll, R. M., & Collins, G. J. (2017). Accountability and control in American schools. *Journal of Curriculum Studies* 49 (1): 75–95. https://doi.org/10.1080/00220272.2016.1205142.

Kayi-Aydar, H. (2015). Teacher agency, positioning, and English language learners: Voices of pre-service classroom teachers. *Teaching and Teacher Education* 45: 94–103. https://doi.org/10.1016/j.tate.2014.09.009.

Kelly, P. (2006). What is teacher learning? A socio-cultural perspective. *Oxford Review of Education* 32 (4): 505–19.

King, P. M., & Kitchener, K. S. (2004). Reflective judgment: Theory and research on the development of epistemic assumptions through adulthood. *Educational Psychologist* 39 (1): 5–18. https://doi.org/10.1207/s15326985ep3901_2.

Knowles, M. S. (1988). *The modern practice of adult education: From pedagogy to andragogy*. Revised ed. Englewood Cliffs, NJ: Cambridge Book Company.

LaBoskey, V. K. (2009). "'Name it and claim it': The methodology of self-study as social justice teacher education." In L. Fitzgerald, M. Heston, & D. Tidwell (Eds.), *Research methods for the self-study of practice* (pp. 73–82). Dordrecht, Netherlands: Springer. https://doi.org/10.1007/978-1-4020-9514-6_5.

LaGravenese, R. (2007). *Freedom writers*. Paramount.

Lasky, S. (2005). A sociocultural approach to understanding teacher identity, agency and professional vulnerability in a context of secondary school reform. *Teaching and Teacher Education* 21 (8): 899–916.https://doi.org/10.1016/j.tate.2005.06.003.

Lave, J., & Wenger, E. (1991). *Situated learning: Legitimate peripheral participation*. 1st ed. Cambridge: Cambridge University Press.

Leithwood, K., & Jantzi, D. (2006). Transformational school leadership for large-scale reform: Effects on students, teachers, and their classroom practices. *School Effectiveness and School Improvement* 17 (2): 201–27.

Levin, Claudia. (2000). Only a teacher: Teaching timeline. *PBS*. http://www.pbs.org/onlyateacher/timeline.html.

Lipponen, L., & Kumpulainen, K. (2011). Acting as accountable authors: Creating interactional spaces for agency work in teacher education. *Teaching and Teacher Education* 27 (5): 812–19. https://doi.org/10.1016/j.tate.2011.01.001.

Long, C. (2015, May 13). Teacher turnover is much lower than you probably think. *NEA Today*. http://neatoday.org/2015/05/13/teacher-turnover-is-much-lower-than-you-probably-think.

Lortie, D. C. (2002). *Schoolteacher: A sociological study*. 2nd ed. Chicago: University of Chicago Press.

McNiff, J. (2013). *Action research: Principles and practice*. 3rd ed. Milton Park, Canada: Routledge.

Mertler, C. A. (2016). *Action research: Improving schools and empowering educators*. 5th ed. Thousand Oaks, CA: Sage.

Mezirow, J. (1990). *Fostering critical reflection in adulthood: A guide to transformative and emancipatory learning*. 1st ed. San Francisco: Jossey-Bass.

Mezirow, J. (1998). On critical reflection. *Adult Education Quarterly* 48 (3): 185–98. https://doi.org/10.1177/074171369804800305.

Miller, J., Householter, D., & Kasdan, J. (2011). *Bad teacher*. Columbia Pictures.

Murrell, P. C., Diez, M. E., Feiman-Nemser, S., & Schussler, D. (Ed.). (2010). *Teaching as a moral practice: Defining, developing, and assessing professional dispositions in teacher education*. Cambridge, MA: Harvard Education Press.

Musca, T. (Producer), & Menendez, R. (Director). (1988). *Stand and deliver*. Warner Brothers.
Musingafi, M. C. C. & Chiwanza, K. (2014). The classroom situation: Does teaching qualify to be called a profession? *Journal of Education and Literature* 1 (4), 128–32 from http://www.academia.edu/8701287/The_Classroom_Situation_Does_Teaching_Qualify_To_Be_Called_a_Profession
National Center for Education Statistics (2013, June). *The nation's report card: Trends in academic progress 2012*. Washington, DC: Institute of Education Sciences, U.S. Department of Education. https://nces.ed.gov/nationsreportcard/subject/publications/main2012/pdf/2013456.pdf.
NCTAF. (2016a). Teacher shortages: What's the problem? https://nctaf.org/featured-home/teacher-shortages-whats-the-problem.
NCTAF. (2016b). What matters now: A new compact for teaching and learning. https://nctaf.org/wp-content/uploads/2016/08/NCTAF_What-Matters-Now_A-Call-to-Action.pdf.
Nelson, F. L., & Sadler, T. (2012). A third space for reflection by teacher educators: A heuristic for understanding orientations to and components of reflection. *Reflective Practice* 14 (1): 43–57.
Nichols, S. L., & Berliner, D. C. (2007). *Collateral damage: How high-stakes testing corrupts America's schools*. Cambridge, MA: Harvard Education Press.
Nieto, S. (2005). *Why we teach*. New York: Teachers College Press.
Orfield, G., & Lee, C. (2005). *Why segregation matters: Poverty and educational inequality*. Cambridge, MA: Harvard Civil Rights Project.
OECD. (2016). *PISA 2015 results*. Vol. 1: *Excellence and equity in education*. Paris: OECD. http://dx.doi.org/10.1787/9789264266490-en.
Ostorga, A. N., & Estrada, V. L. (2009). Impact of an action research instructional model: Student teachers as reflective thinkers. *Action in Teacher Education* 31 (1): 18–27. http://www.tandfonline.com/doi/abs/10.1080/01626620.2009.10734449#preview.
Pajares, M. F. (1992). Beliefs in educational research: Cleaning up a messy construct. *Review of Educational Research* 62 (3): 307–32.
Palmer, P. J. (2007). *The courage to teach: Exploring the inner landscape of a teacher's life*. Hoboken, NJ: Jossey Bass.
Passion. *Merriam-Webster*. (2017). https://www.merriam-webster.com/dictionary/passion.
Payne, C. (2017, March 23). "The limits of schooling: The power of poverty." Centennial lecture presented at the American Educational Research Association (webinar). https://www.youtube.com/watch?v=jexJl8iqTqI.
Pease-Alvarez, L., & Samway, K. D. (2012). *Teachers of English learners negotiating authoritarian policies*. Dordrecht, Netherlands: Springer Science and Business Media.
Priestley, M., Biesta, G., & Robinson, S. (2015). *Teacher agency: An ecological approach*. London: Bloomsbury Academic.
Ravitch, D. (2010). *The death and life of the great American school system: How testing and choice are undermining education*. New York: Basic Books.
Reed, M. (2003). "The agency/structure dilemma in organizational theory." In H. Tsoukas & C. Knudsen (Eds.), *The Oxford handbook of organization theory: Meta-theoretical perspectives*. Revised ed. New York: Oxford University Press.
Richmond, E. (2012, April 18). Should teachers get bonuses for student achievement? *The Atlantic*. Retrieved from https://www.theatlantic.com/national/archive/2012/04/should-teachers-get-bonuses-for-student-achievement/256075/
Rogers, C. R., & Freiberg, H. J. (1994). *Freedom to learn*. 3rd ed. New York: Pearson.
Roth, W.-M., & Lee, Y.-J. (2007). "Vygotsky's neglected legacy": Cultural-historical activity theory. *Review of Educational Research* 77 (2): 186–232. https://doi.org/10.3102/0034654306298273.
Saunders, M., Alcantara, V., Cervantes, L., Del Razo, J., López, R., & Perez, W. (2017). *Getting to teacher ownership: How schools are creating meaningful change, executive summary*. Providence, RI: Brown University, Annenberg Institute for School Reform.
Shohamy, E. (2009). Language teachers as partners in crafting educational language policies? *Íkala, Revista de Lenguaje Y Cultura* 14 (22): 45–67.

# References

Schön, D. A. (1984). *The reflective practitioner: How professionals think in action.* New York: Basic Books.
Spillane, J. P. (2012). *Distributed leadership.* San Francisco: John Wiley and Sons.
Stinson, E. (2005). "Teaching outside the lines." In S. Nieto (Ed.), *Why We Teach* (pp. 105–13). New York: Teachers College.
Taylor, G., & Runté, R. (1995). *Thinking about teaching: An introduction.* Toronto: Harcourt Brace.
Teacher-Powered Schools. (2017). School inventory. https://www.teacherpowered.org/inventory.
TESOL International Association. (2013, March). *Overview of the common core state standards initiatives for ELLs.* Alexandria, VA: Author.
Trigg, R. (2001). *Understanding social science.* 2nd ed. Oxford: Blackwell.
Tucker, M. (2017, September 14). Teachers' pay: What on Earth are we thinking? *Education Week.* http://blogs.edweek.org/edweek/top_performers/2017/09/teachers_pay_what_on_earth_are_we_thinking.html.
U.S. Department of Education. (2013). Institute of Education Sciences, National Center for Education Statistics, National Assessment of Educational Progress (NAEP), 2009, 2011, and 2015 science assessments.
U.S. Department of Education. (2016). *The state of racial diversity in the educator workforce.* Washington, DC: Office of Planning, Evaluation and Policy Development, Policy and Program Studies Service. https://www.nationsreportcard.gov/science_2015/files/overview.pdf.
U.S. News (2015, September 21). As test results trickle in, states still ditching common core. http://www.usnews.com/news/articles/2015/09/21/as-test-results-trickle-in-states-still-ditching-common-core.
Villalba, A. (1990). Institutional organization in educational facilitation. *Journal of Educational Facilitation* (1): 33–45.
Villegas-Reimers, E., & Reimers, F. (1996). Where are 60 million teachers? The missing voice in educational reforms around the world. *Prospects* 26: 469–92.
Vygotsky, L. S. (1978). Interaction between learning and development. *Readings on the development of children* 23 (3): 34–41.
Vygotsky, L. S. (1980). *Mind in society: The development of higher psychological processes.* Cambridge, MA: Harvard University Press.
Walker, T. (2014, September 22). The long history of blaming teachers first. *NEA Today.* http://neatoday.org/2014/09/22/the-long-history-of-blaming-teachers-first.
Walker, T. (2016, August 16). Report: Teacher pay penalty growing more severe. *NEA Today.* http://neatoday.org/2016/08/16/teacher-pay-penalty.
Walsh, D. (1998). Structure/agency. In C. Jencs (Ed.), *Core sociological dichotomies.* London: Sage.
Weber, E. (2007). Globalization, "global" development, and teachers' work: A research agenda. *Review of Educational Research* 77 (3): 279–309.
Wenger, E. (1999). *Communities of practice: Learning, meaning, and identity.* 1st ed. Cambridge: Cambridge University Press.
Wenger, E., McDermott, R. A., & Snyder, W. (2002). *Cultivating communities of practice: A guide to managing knowledge.* Boston: Harvard Business Press.
Wertsch, J. V. (1993). *Voices of the mind.* Cambridge, MA: Harvard University Press.
Wertsch, J. V., Tulviste, P., & Hagstrom, F. (1993). "A sociocultural approach to agency." In E. A. Forman, N. Minick, & C. A. Stone (Eds.), *Contexts for learning: Sociocultural dynamics in children's development* (pp. 336–56). Revised ed. New York: Oxford University Press.
Winerip, M. (2011, April 11). Reflections on the relevance of schools chancellors. *New York Times.* http://wirednewyork.com/forum/archive/index.php/t-24295.html?s=08035c062164f4e93d2f8d853a4a0573.
Wink, J. (2000). *Critical pedagogy: Notes from the real world.* 2nd ed. Boston: Pearson.
Yasnitsky, A., Veer, R., & Ferrari, M. (Eds.). (2014). *The Cambridge handbook of cultural-historical psychology.* Cambridge: Cambridge University Press.

Yoon, K. S., Duncan, T., Lee, S. W.-Y., Scarloss, B., & Shapley, K. (2007). Reviewing the evidence on how teacher professional development affects student achievement (Issues & Answers Report, REL 2007–No. 033). Washington, DC: U.S. Department of Education, Institute of Education Sciences, National Center for Education Evaluation and Regional Assistance, Regional Educational Laboratory Southwest. Retrieved from http://ies.ed.gov/ncee/edlabs

Zeichner, K. M., & Liston, D. P. (1996). Reflective teaching: An introduction. *Harvard Educational Review* 57 (1): 23–48.

# Index

accountability, 3, 5, 18, 19, 21, 36, 41, 54, 81
accountability movement, xi, 19
action research, 64, 65, 67, 76, 86; proactive action, 65; reflective practice, 64
activism, 13, 16, 17, 82, 83
adult development, 29
adult Learning theory, xvi, 25, 26, 28, 73, 74
agency structure paradigm, xiv, xv, xvi; conflationism, xv; determinism, xiv; reductionist approach/reductionism, xiv; relationism/realism, xiv; within school structure, xiv
as art or science, xii, 9
authoritative, xvi, 63
autonomy, xi, xii, xiii, 3, 5, 32, 35, 44, 52, 76

CHAT. *See* cultural historical activity theory
common schools, 14
communities of practice, 31, 33, 80
conscientization, 39, 40, 83, 84, 85, 86
cultural historical activity theory, 37, 38, 39
cultural-historical theory, 25, 31, 33, 36, 37, 40, 73
critical pedagogy, vii, xvii, 1, 24, 25, 28, 39, 40, 69, 73, 74, 84

development in context, 32
Dewey, J., 17
Dirkswager, E.J., 1, 12, 32, 34, 35, 38, 81, 82
diversity in teaching force, 10, 23, 24, 72, 73

Edwards, A., 34, 38, 82

Farris-Berg, K., 1, 12, 32, 34, 35, 38, 81, 82
Freire, P., 25, 39, 69, 70, 74, 82

Junge, A., 1, 12, 32, 34, 35, 38, 81, 82

Lasky, S., 36, 37

Mann, H., 14, 15, 22
Mezirow, J., 26, 28, 29, 30, 31, 74, 82

networking, 67

positioning theory, 34
positionality, 32, 35, 67
profession, teaching as, 5, 7, 8, 13, 15, 21, 22; structural functionalism, 7; trait model, 7, 8
professional development, x, 5, 15, 31, 33, 34, 59, 63, 66, 72, 73, 76
professional identity, 25, 33, 34, 35, 36, 39, 40, 41, 42, 60, 61, 62, 75, 79, 82

professionalization of teaching, 8, 9, 17, 19
professional talk, 63, 64
progressivism, 17, 18

Reed, M., xiv, xv
reflection, 29; critical reflection, 29, 30, 31, 74, 82, 83, 84, 86; critical thinking, 18, 84
Runté, G., 7, 8

sociocultural theory, xv

Taylor, G., 7, 8
teacher attrition, xi, xvi, 21, 72
teacher identity, xvi, 36, 61, 69
teacher leadership, 3, 77, 78
teacher ownership, 81, 87
teacher training, 28
teacher unions, 16, 17, 21
transformative learning, 30, 31

Wenger, E., 31, 33, 78, 80
Wink, J., 39, 83

# About the Author and Contributor

**Alcione Negrão Ostorga** is an associate professor at the University of Texas, Rio Grande Valley, in the Department of Bilingual and Literacy Studies, where she works as a teacher educator at the graduate and undergraduate levels. She has more than thirty-five years of experience as an educator.

Prior to being a teacher educator, she was an elementary school teacher for ten years, where she taught fifth grade and also worked with special education students. As a mother and community member, she was one of the cofounders of the Cypress Hills Community School, P.S. 89, a public school in New York City where parents play a key role in the decision-making process of the school. This school is led by two administrators, an educator codirector (principal) and a parent codirector. A central feature of the school is a dual-language program in Spanish and English.

Her research focus has been on the development of professional identities, reflective practices, and teacher action research through the application of adult learning and sociocultural learning theories, as well as preparation of teachers of Latinx cultural backgrounds. She is also conducting research toward the development of a border pedagogy for teacher preparation. She views the elements of professional identities, reflective practices, action research, and the border pedagogy for Latinx preservice teachers as important components in the development of teacher agency.

**Lileana Ríos-Ledezma** is a bilingual/ESL instructional coach for a school district in central Texas. During her ten years in education, she has worked as a bilingual teacher, a lead teacher, and an instructional coach in several school districts in the Rio Grande Valley and now in the Bryan/College Station area. She received her bachelor's and master's degrees from the University of Texas, Pan-American (now known as University of Texas, Rio

Grande Valley). She is pursuing a PhD in educational psychology with a specialization in bilingual education at Texas A&M University.

www.ingramcontent.com/pod-product-compliance
Lightning Source LLC
Chambersburg PA
CBHW032030230426
43671CB00005B/257